ADVANCE PRAISE

"Great insight and inspiring little bite-sized snippets of life and business wisdom. I couldn't stop reading them!"

—DEREK SIVERS, AUTHOR OF *ANYTHING YOU WANT*, AND FOUNDER OF CD BABY, THE MOST POPULAR MUSIC SITE FOR INDEPENDENT ARTISTS

"Successful firms share a common trait of bringing intentionality and caring to their team, clients, and products/services. In Day-In, Day-Out, Nicholas shares how he and his wife applied these principles both at home and in successfully scaling their business."

—VERNE HARNISH, AUTHOR OF *SCALING UP (ROCKEFELLER HABITS 2.0)* AND FOUNDER OF ENTREPRENEURS' ORGANIZATION (EO)

"Day-In, Day-Out is more than just a guidebook for business owners; it's an important resource for anyone who wants to turn their dream into a reality. The insights provided by

Nick Dancer are many of the same ones I used while growing Sweetwater from the back of my VW bus. Hard work, determination, and perseverance pay off, as does a commitment to doing the right thing. Readers of Day-In, Day-Out will learn how to apply those invaluable principles to their own lives."

—CHUCK SURACK, FOUNDER AND
CEO, SWEETWATER SOUND

"Day In, Day Out is down to earth, elegant, totally practical, well-buffed, and a multi-faceted work that contributes to the quality of the reader's life much more than a quick casual observer is likely to realize. While one could certainly get away with less well-rounded business advice, anyone who takes the long-term, high-quality, ethically responsible approach to business and life will absolutely want to read Nick's great new book."

—ARI WEINZWEIG, CO-FOUNDER OF ZINGERMAN'S
COMMUNITY OF BUSINESSES, AUTHOR OF
ZINGERMAN'S GUIDE TO GOOD LEADING,
PART 1: BUILDING A GREAT BUSINESS

"Day In, Day Out is filled with practical and simple messages that help to navigate life—both personally and professionally. Nick teaches us that life doesn't need to be complicated. Simply show up, be practical, do the work, and the rest will take care of itself."

—ROB DUBE, CO-FOUNDER AND PRESIDENT OF
IMAGEONE, AND AUTHOR OF THE BOOK DONOTHING

DAY IN, DAY OUT

DAY IN, DAY OUT

THE SECRET POWER IN SHOWING UP AND DOING THE WORK

NICHOLAS DANCER

LIONCREST
PUBLISHING

DAY IN, DAY OUT
The Secret Power in Showing Up and Doing the Work

ISBN 978-1-5445-0274-8 *Paperback*
978-1-5445-0273-1 *Ebook*

Cover Design by Alexis Dancer, ArtC
Sketches by Ben Doege
Author Photo by Allison Gray

To my wife, Alexis, the love of my life.

And my three boys, Clark, Charles, and Clyde.

CONTENTS

INTRODUCTION

One of the first self-improvement books I ever read was Napoleon Hill's 1937 timeless classic *Think and Grow Rich*. I was nineteen when I first picked it up, and it changed the way I thought. It showed me the possibility of something more. It told me I could be creative—that deep inside me, and inside you, is creativity that can change our lives if it's harnessed and put to work.

I continued to find more books that would guide me along this new path—books on spiritual development, physical fitness, leadership, being your most authentic self, relationships, and business. Even though each book covered a different topic, they all seemed to lead back to the same key principles—principles derived from spiritual truths, natural laws, or ancient wisdom. Each author offered a unique perspective on these. Each of them also championed the notion that while none of us can control

Our first samples were stained and finished in our bathtub. We have so many stories like that.

The business was never just about me; although I started the company, there have been many people who have come and gone, or who are still with the company. These people have contributed, have helped us grow, and have helped us get better and better.

Today, a decade later, we have grown into a team of eighteen people. We run and operate everything together. We do millions of dollars worth of work each year. To some, this might seem amazing, and to others it's small potatoes. But for me, it simply works. I love that my role is now a blend of leading and training our team, building systems, bringing in new bidding opportunities, and being covered in dust and sludge as I help with 'installs.'

We are a niche business specializing in polished concrete and epoxy floor coatings. We physically change the design, the feel, and the impact on interior spaces. We say that "we install floors for the modern world," which means we get to work in the hippest retail spaces, in schools and universities, in high-end commercial buildings, and in industrial and manufacturing facilities where everything from aluminum car parts to furniture is made.

My business is just one of many examples that show

you don't need to be the next Google to run a successful business today. You don't need to raise money, have all the fancy titles, or have a bunch of crazy benefits. We take care of our people, but we don't need nap pods to be successful. We keep things simple. We believe in positively impacting every space we enter and every person we encounter by doing our best work.

AUTHENTIC ALL THE WAY THROUGH

Rather than separate yourself from your work, what if you thought of all aspects of your life as inextricably connected? If you make your business your life's work, you don't have to shut off one part of your life to turn on the other. Your authentic self is able to flow all the way through, making your success in each realm success in the other.

If you ask me how I built Dancer Concrete Design from the ground up, I would tell you I showed up and did the work. Day in and day out, I physically showed up and devoted all of my energy to it. Though some of my functions have changed as we have grown, I still view everything I do the same way. I still use the same principles in business that I use to build and improve the rest of my life.

Although each chapter in this book focuses on a particular principle, not all are specific to business. That's why I would not classify *Day In, Day Out* as a business book per se. Rather, it's a life book, containing principles that can help drive transformation in your business *and* your life.

I have written this book for anyone who is tired of trying to cheat or hack their way to results in short periods of time. This is for anyone who understands that great things need time to mature and develop. This is for anyone who wants something different than the 'quick fix' or 'make it happen' bravo that floods the business book section.

This is for you if you're a small-business owner, someone who wants to start a small business, or someone who desires to go after something big—not just a single goal you want to reach, but something you have to maintain as well. This is for you if you want to work *in* and *on* your business; you consider your business your life's work. This is for you if you are fully committed to your work, your duty, and your purpose.

Day In, Day Out is not for people who want to work on their laptop from a beach somewhere as they travel the world, occasionally checking in to see how their business is doing. This book is for those who want to give everything they have to *what* they build and to the people *with* and *for whom* they build it. It's for people who want to build something great while understanding what greatness actually is.

In his book, *A New Earth*, Eckhart Tolle says:

> The great arises out of small things that are honored and cared for. Greatness is a mental abstraction and a favorite fantasy of the ego. The paradox is that the foundation for greatness is honoring the small things of the present moment instead of pursuing the idea of greatness.[1]

Greatness is not a goal—it's a way of life. Only when we learn the greatness of the mundane will we discover a truly great life.

A NOTE ON BORROWING

In his book *Steal Like an Artist*, Austin Kleon shares his theory that there is no new art. There are different perspectives, certainly, but in the end, it's all the same. Even the masterpieces are repeated and repeatable. My goal is to share principles others have used, I have used, and you can use, too.

None of the principles discussed in this book are original to me. I have simply borrowed them and put them to use. When I come across a new idea or see a principle at work

---

1   Tolle, Eckhart. *A New Earth: Awakening Your Life's Purpose*. New York: Penguin Books, 2016.

PART I

MOVE

Move is about movement. All adventures start with movement, with action. It's the moving that gets the work done. Moving forward is the only way to keep from going backward.

THE WAY

Pick a path.

One of the most critical components of every journey is deciding which way to go. Traveling 500 miles north from my current location lands me in the middle of some Canadian wilderness. In the winter, the ground might be covered with snow, and I might see a moose. Five hundred miles south gets me to a warm, sunny day in downtown Nashville, Tennessee. There, I might find myself in a café, listening to an up-and-coming artist. It's 500 miles either way, but the direction I take gets me to extremely different results.

It's no different in business. The leaders and team of Zingerman's, a small, gourmet food company in Ann Arbor, Michigan, understood this truth. Founders, Ari Weinzweig and Paul Saginaw, decided on a defined path and stuck to it.

As their company grew, it was featured in Bo Burlingham's book, *Small Giants*, and also featured as one of *Inc.* magazine's most successful small businesses in America. Zingerman's garnered so much attention that the founders received offers to franchise into other markets and branch out into other business models. But instead of following the money, they stuck to their vision.

What was their vision? To be in close proximity to all aspects of the business so they could grow their people and deliver the best product. If an outside offer didn't align with the path they had chosen, they simply said no. Weinzweig once commented, "I don't want to travel halfway around the world to see some less-than-great version of our business."[2] The founders decided they want to have a more 'hands on' approach in their organization. They believe that in order to deliver the best, proximity is important.

Early on, the way was chosen—where Zingerman's would operate, whom they would serve, and how they would grow. To this day, the founders are still on the path they defined from the outset. Even with over sixty million dol-

---

2   Burlingham, Bo. *Small Giants: Companies That Choose to Be Great Instead of Big*. New York: Penguin Group, 2005.

lars in sales from their twelve sub-organizations, which they call their 'community of businesses,' they have stayed true to their path. In fact, Ari still serves regularly at their restaurant, The Roadhouse. Seriously, you can go there and say hello to him.

KEEP YOUR OPTIONS ~~OPEN~~ CLOSED

Keeping your options open seems wise, doesn't it? If your plan doesn't work out, you want to have a backup, right? Perhaps. But in a world of endless possibilities, keeping your options open can stop you from making any decision at all. And indecision is worse than no decision.

As you read about Zingerman's and the choice they made, do you find yourself attracted to their business? Do you think, *Dang, I want to run a business like that.* Well, I would guess that it's not the specific path they chose that draws you in—it's their intention. Because they keep their options closed, they can focus on the specific things they care about.

Their decision to stay local in Ann Arbor doesn't mean it's the 'right' decision; it's just the right decision for them. They could sell their famous Rueben Sandwich all over the country, and it would sell well. But they believe they can produce the best sandwich in Ann Arbor, so they stay put. That's courage in action.

Your life needs a direction, and direction starts with a single decision. By choosing a direction, you will be positioned to make clearer decisions today and each day moving forward.

YOUR PATH AND YOUR POTENTIAL

To follow the way you have chosen, you must also be self-aware. Ask yourself: *Where am I right now, and where do I want to be?* Through constant self-awareness, you can stay on your path as you move toward your potential.

Perhaps you're ready to take your business to the next level. You've analyzed the market and know it allows for growth, and you're ready to do the focused work required to grow. Great! This isn't the time to change directions on a whim every other day. This isn't the time to let the latest news story about a hot new market entice you to jump ship and chase down ghosts. This is a time to keep the path to your potential crystal clear.

In our business, I've made the path to our potential as crystal clear as possible for myself and my team. I believe our company will be at its best with a staff of about forty working at facilities in several cities within close proximity; this will enable us to have a regional impact, while our local staff won't have to travel as much. I have no interest in expanding nationally; that's not part of the vision.

Flying in a plane to polish a floor in Oregon sounds fun, until I get on the plane and wish I could just work down the street.

While we move toward our potential, my focus is to establish a business with a great reputation that does solid, market-leading work. I say no to any offers that come along if they don't align with this path. I don't want to get involved in other services, because they don't support our vision. They would only distract us.

For Dancer Concrete Design, the way is clear: to maintain the highest quality in polished concrete and epoxy floor services. To be the best in what we do. The way doesn't always sound super sexy, but it works for me.

Leave trying to do everything to Amazon. Find a path where you can be the best.

BRAD AND DINKY (GO ALL THE WAY)

While at my local YMCA, I happened to be on the rower and noticed two other guys who seemed to be friends working out together. For this story's purpose, let's call them Brad (sounds like a strong name) and Dinky (sounds, well...not strong).

They each had a set of dumbbells in their hands, and Brad was leading an exercise of front lunges across the room. Down—Up. Down—Up. It was clear that Brad works out regularly. He was a solid 180 pounds of muscle at 5'10". But he didn't just look strong; he also focused on his movement. His lunges were smooth, and in every single movement, his knee would softly touch the ground and come back up. It was evident Brad was performing the move correctly.

Behind him came Dinky. Probably a lovable pal, Dinky took a different view on his exercise. Dinky sometimes touched his knee on the ground, and sometimes didn't. He probably had good intentions, but he wasn't fully focused. He seemed to approach the exercise with an *if it happens, it happens* mentality.

Dinky was also not too focused on completing his rounds. Instead of executing the exercise all the way to the wall like Brad did, he stopped about five feet short with a lackluster last lunge and then scooted over to the wall, signaling that he was complete with the set and that Brad could start his next set.

With his back up against the wall, Brad put his right foot forward and begun to lunge back from where he came. Once Brad was five to six lunges ahead, it was now time for Dinky to start. Do you think he started with his back against the wall to make sure he did the full exercise? Na, not so much.

Dinky had other plans. He awkwardly stumbled forward about three steps and then started his set, just as sloppy as before, this time cutting his work short by a few lunges at the outset.

ARE YOU PLAYING ALL OUT?

Now before you start judging me and telling me, "Hey, not everyone can be as strong as Brad" or "Maybe it was one of Dinky's first times working out," stick with me.

The truth is that Dinky was just sloppy. He wanted the easy way out. When things got tough, he cut corners, skipped reps, and did sloppy work. And you know what? His rewards for that workout are going to be minimal, and he is not going to understand that because he thinks he works out just as much as Brad. He's going to say Brad just has a stronger build, that Brad has better genes, eats the right food, or he'll come up with other excuses about why he's not getting the results Brad is.

The truth is that Brad is getting stronger with his workout because he is doing it the right way. Dinky is just going through the motions, and so he will not get any stronger. They might spend the same time, but Brad gets the reward, while Dinky simply wastes an hour.

I have been a Dinky. I tried to be a Dinky in my workouts, in my business, in my marriage, and as a dad. I slacked in almost every part of my life. I went through the motions. I looked for easier ways to do everything. *I can do it differently*, I thought. *I can get the same results in an easier and softer way.* While everyone else was showing up and doing the full work, I thought I could shortcut my way through.

But it doesn't work that way. When I was playing the lack-luster game instead of playing all out, I was too focused on what was next instead of what was right in front of me.

We all have a little bit of Dinky inside of us, the part of us that wants to take the easy way out. But while we Dinky our way through life, the Brads of the world are hard at work, embracing the pain, doing things well, and reaping the rewards.

It's easy to look at the Brads and think, *Well, he must have good genes,* or *I don't have the experience he has.* But we know those are just excuses. The Brads show up every day and do the work with discipline, fortitude, and intention. They consistently make the decision to improve.

Be that person. Be a Brad. Be the stronger version of you.

DRAMA POINTS

Imagine that you have a leaky faucet in your house. Your spouse has reminded you of it several times and for the last few weeks, you have been able to put it off. But this coming weekend, you have some time and think you can fix it. The project is just small enough that you think the charge for a plumber is too much, so you decide to do it yourself. How hard can it be, right?

With a cup of coffee in hand, you watch an online video of easy plumbing fixes, plan a material list, and head to the local home supply store. You pick out a few shiny new tools, twenty dollars' worth of PVC pipe in various shapes, and head for home to master your domain.

Once home, you execute a few contortionist moves to get under the sink. It's not until you take everything apart that you realize you forgot the thread tape. You mutter a litany of blue language, but you know the pipes will leak again without the tape. Your only option is to drive back to the store, adding another hour to the project. You made a checklist this morning, and this extra trip was not planned. You need to spend extra time and resources, but the project doesn't make any additional progress. Instead, things stop while you head back.

By the time you're back to the house the second time, the water has been shut off for half of the day. The 'easy' plumbing fix has turned into a daylong debacle. The additional trip is an example of what I call a 'drama point.'

CHARTING THE EFFECTS

A drama point is that time in space where you are working harder or adding resources, but the results out don't line up with input or work in. Drama points are pesky intruders, and worst of all, they're almost always unavoidable.

In lean business operations, drama points equal waste. If one of our team members drives to a worksite an hour away and only then realizes he forgot a special tool, he needs to drive all the way back. This creates a drama point. The extra trip adds extra transportation and extra work. We're putting in extra time and energy, but ultimately achieving the same, or less, results.

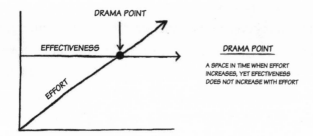

DRAMA POINT

DRAMA POINT

A SPACE IN TIME WHEN EFFORT
INCREASES, YET EFECTIVENESS
DOES NOT INCREASE WITH EFFORT

RESPONDING

We can't fully eliminate drama points in our lives, and getting frustrated by them usually makes matters worse. So, what can we do? We can recognize common drama points and minimize them as much as possible.

Today, you can commit to spending time identifying the most common drama points in your life. Your most common drama point might only cause a ten-minute delay, but if you know it happens multiple times a week, you can see the bigger picture of how much time you waste.

You might add a checklist to a process. You might spend two hours organizing your tools so that you don't have that ten-minute delay. By taking this simple step to identify and minimize drama points, you'll be able to focus more on results and less on putting out fires.

RESULTS

In our business, I noticed that one of our machines consistently broke down on the job. We still had our daily goals to reach, but every time the machine broke down, we spent an extra two hours fixing it. Our eight-hour day turned into a ten-hour day, but we ultimately did the same amount of work. In other words, we worked for ten hours, with eight hours of output. The machine breaking was the drama point that shifted our progress.

Eventually, we realized that we needed to spend a little extra time fixing this common drama point that was sucking up our resources. We can't solve every little problem we have, but we could solve this recurring issue. Instead of just working on machines when they broke, we added a process to our work, so the machines would go through a breakdown and cleaning after each job.

We didn't initially want to add this maintenance procedure because of the time it takes to break down one of our machines. But eventually, we realized it was worth investing in the up-front cost of doing more maintenance rather than reacting, rushing, and overnighting parts when something broke. The maintenance is now planned, and time is allowed for changing parts and greasing. Sometimes we spend the time to take apart a machine and find that it doesn't need any work done to it.

But it's still better to take it apart in our time than to tear one down on a site and hold up a whole project.

AN UNAVOIDABLE REALITY

Ultimately, your goal is to eliminate drama points as much as possible. However, some drama points are unavoidable.

For example, you might find that certain areas of your life consistently have a lot of drama points, and you can't avoid spending time or energy on them no matter what you do. For me, plumbing is one of those areas of life. Whenever I have a plumbing problem in my house, I now leave it to the experts. I know that the cost to hire a plumber is high, but I've also crawled under the sink with a wrench one too many times, only to waste half of the day.

In many areas of life, you won't be able to predict drama points at all. The only way to respond to this reality is to acknowledge it and to factor in a bit more time, energy, and resources into all your efforts, whatever they might be.

STAYING AWAY FROM EXTREMES

Red Bull uses video to show us what extreme looks like. Extreme looks like jumping off a cliff somewhere with a wingsuit and trying to fly like a bird. Or it looks like building some enormous ramp and having someone on a bike, snowboard, or some wheeled device go off of it and hang in the air for what seems like a record amount of time, only to land safely with the crowd cheering. Watching these videos, it's only natural to say, "Wow!"

The more advertising we see that depicts extremes, the more we start to believe that extremes are normal and sustainable—that if we really want to be the best, we just have to do crazy things like that. But that's not true. In fact, the secret to most successful growth lies in a progression of steady, effective, and harmonious days. Some might call this boring, but if you have the ability to stay steady, even when things seem boring and even when you don't see results right away, you will ultimately win.

Pick any of the world's most successful and widely known companies today. If you track back through their history, you will see that they were not built overnight. To have lasting results in any area of life, including business, you stay away from extremes. You build a sustainable rhythm and stick to it day in and day out.

CHARTING EXTREMES

Life works according to balances. The universe always has a counterbalance, and a corresponding shift is required in the negative space. If you think working eighteen-hour days is the answer for you, that's great. But do it seven days a week, and you might find a big crash is in your future.

In the following chart, we see the relationship between extreme life shifts and ensuing crashes. To live in those extremes, you not only need a tremendous amount of energy to keep going, but you need a lot more energy to get going after a crash if you want to reach the same goal. You have to expend much more energy by going too hard, too fast.

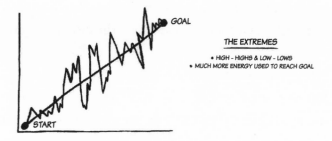

THE EXTREMES

- HIGH - HIGHS & LOW - LOWS
- MUCH MORE ENERGY USED TO REACH GOAL

By steadily progressing, however, you can reach a goal with much less effort, without needing to waste energy digging out of unexpected holes. To stay above the lows and keep climbing, you eliminate extremes.

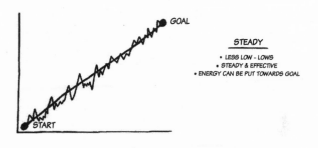

STEADY

- LESS LOW - LOWS
- STEADY & EFFECTIVE
- ENERGY CAN BE PUT TOWARDS GOAL

The key to lasting results is to use your own discipline to keep growing, not try to ride a wave of an extreme and hope you come out the other side intact.

"WORK/LIFE BALANCE"

In his book *The ONE Thing*, Gary Keller offers his take on work/life balance. He argues that to be most productive, you actually have to have balance between your work and other parts of life.[3]

It's not realistic to think you can always maintain a perfect work/life balance. One week, you might need to spend extra hours completing a proposal for a client. The next week, a kid is sick and you need to spend more time at home.

Each time one of our children was born, I took off extra time from work to be at home. I chose to do this, but I also knew that the choice would come at a cost to the business. Whenever I need to put in extra time at work, on the other hand, I need to know how that will affect my family so that I'm prepared ahead of time.

Along the way, what is important is to realize how movement in any one direction will affect the overall balance of your life.

---

3   Keller, Gary and Papasan, Jay. *The ONE Thing: The Surprisingly Simple Truth Behind Extraordinary Results*. Austin, TX: Bard Press, 2013.

SHOOT FOR THE STARS, BUT DON'T MISS THE TARGET

Bookstore shelves are filled with feel-good motivational stories that urge entrepreneurs and executives to shoot for the stars and work like crazy to achieve everything right away. *Sleep in your office if you have to. Pull all-nighters all the time.*

But those extremes come at a cost. I tried that life of extremes for a little while. I tried to sleep at the office for a few nights because I thought that's what small business owners have to do. But when I looked more closely, I quickly realized that extremes always came at a cost. I lacked in my ability to plan and had zero rhythm to the day.

Many people also add too many extremes on top of each other. Imagine starting brand new eating habits. As soon as you start feeling good, you add in a new exercise routine as well. *Just an hour a day*, you think. Within a week, you've completely changed your eating habits and are in the gym more than you have ever been before. *Big changes ahead with this quick ramp up*, you think. It would come as no surprise if within a couple of weeks, you simply can't maintain the pace and find yourself putting pizza rolls in the oven and binge-watching Netflix. Again, the balance of life would kick in.

Take a moment to think about it. How many times have you found yourself feeling great about a new change or challenge, but then lost steam and were unable to move forward? Have you ever wondered why a pattern keeps repeating itself?

By stepping back for a moment and giving yourself more space to be realistic about extremes, you can focus on one goal at a time. In turn, you might find that you reach more stars than you expected you would.

THE MYTH OF CHAOS

We generally believe creativity *requires* some level of chaos. We might imagine our artistic friend living in a completely chaotic environment, paint cans strewn across the floor and nothing put away. "My mind works better this way," they say. We nod in understanding. This is the cost of being a creative, right?

But perhaps things aren't that cut and dried. Perhaps within order, we actually free ourselves to be more creative too—not simply to do the dry tasks required to get things done.

French novelist Gustave Flaubert is reported as once saying, "Be structured and well-ordered in life so you can be fierce and original in work."[4] Within his statement,

---

4   Scott, Susan. *Fierce Conversations: Achieving Success at Work and in Life One Conversation at a Time.* New York: Random House, 2017.

he recognized that chaos is a reality of life, but that by controlling what you can and keeping organized, you set yourself up to do better work.

In business, you can deal with a certain amount of chaos when you're small. But as your company grows, you'll need to implement greater order, if only to be respectful to others. Nobody wants to work in someone else's mess. Respond to the reality of chaos by ordering your world, and your entire team will be liberated to be fierce and original in their work.

Keep it neat, clean, and organized.

SHOW UP

"Just press play."

If you have ever popped in the popular P90X workout program, you will notice all sorts of Tony Horton-isms, one of them being "Just Press Play." Tony Horton bases his popular program on this simple but effective statement. He encourages people to simply show up every day, even when they don't feel like it.

The first few P90X workouts are fun. You are learning something new, and your motivation is still high for those first couple of days. You're excited about the sexy new body you are creating. But your third week in, maybe you eat donuts for breakfast and are feeling sluggish. Since you're also still sore from the last workout, you rationalize that you have been doing 'so good' and deserve an extra rest day.

We all rationalize that way. Our minds are funny like that. But what happens when you hear Tony Horton calling you in the back of your mind. He knew this day would come, which is why he's snuck in this message in the workout several times. "Just Press Play," he says. "Even on the day when you don't feel like it. Even when you are sore. Just Press Play."

Tony might as well be a fortune-teller because he can already see the future. If you show up and Just Press Play, the workout will start. Even if you just manage to sit and watch the workout program, you'll have a hard time not getting up at some point and being active. Maybe instead of doing fifty pushups, you manage ten. Heck, maybe you skip the whole first round and just lay on the couch.

But you showed up. And you've kept your habit. It might have been your laziest workout, but you showed up. You kept the momentum alive.

WHAT'S WORTH DOING?

We're all familiar with the phrase, "If it's worth doing, it's worth doing right." Acclaimed author and entrepreneur Keith Cunningham switches things up and says, "If it's worth doing, it's worth doing wrong at first."[5]

---

5   Cunningham, Keith J. *The Road Less Stupid: Advice from the Chairman of the Board.* United States: Keith J. Cunningham, 2018.

Of course, the idea of just showing up is no excuse for doing shoddy work. But if you're doing your best with the energy, knowledge, and skills you have right now, your effort is valuable and meaningful.

In our business, we are more concerned with making progress than doing things perfectly. Sure, doing things perfectly feels great, but perfectionism often keeps us from getting started in the first place. If you wait for perfect, things seem to never actually get done.

Our company has grown, in large part, simply because we show up for our customers. We're there when we say we will be and do what we say we'll do. (Yup, that's our secret. Seriously. It sounds simple, but try it out. Just show up over and over and over again.) Our clients gain nothing if we're excellent one day and then don't show up the next. We show up every day.

Press play and get to work. Keep showing up.

LEAD. IT'S NOT ABOUT BEING IN FRONT.

As we were leaving the church on our bikes, I told the boys that Charlie was going to lead us out of the parking lot. He knows the direction and would be proud to be called the 'leader'—to be out in front of his brother and me. But Clark wanted to be first. He wanted to be the leader, and in his drive to be first, he pushed Charlie to cut him off so he could be out front.

I was frustrated and disappointed at the same time. I was frustrated because Charlie didn't have his chance to take that front role, and I was disappointed in Clark that he didn't understand that leadership is so much more than being in front.

But it wasn't Clark's fault; it was mine. It's my role as their dad to teach them, to show them, to be an example to my boys of what real leadership is.

I also need to be this example at work. Our business is too large to have one leader. It needs many leaders to function and serve our clients.

LEADING IS SERVING OTHERS

Sometimes Clark, Charlie, and I go to the park. Typically, the boys will ride their bikes, while I run with a stroller (as a backup plan).

In our group dynamic, I am the dad and naturally the leader of our group. My role is to set the direction, keep the pace, help them be better bike riders, encourage them when they feel tired, guide them through difficult terrain, and teach them what I know.

I lead them first by serving them. But during this trip, I lead in many other ways too.

SET DIRECTION

We set off for the park. Everyone knows where we are going.

The boys know that when we get there, we get to play.

We make several turns, and as we approach one, I will mention we are taking a left or right.

GO IN FRONT, WHEN NEEDED

As we approach the road to cross the street, I go to the middle of the road to signify to approaching cars that we are passing. I take the lead to protect the boys as they cross the street.

TEACH

When we approach the 'secret passage' (a small wooded trail between a parking lot and the bike trail), I again look ahead to make sure other riders are not coming and slow down to help Charlie through the terrain.

When his bike gets stuck from jumping over the curb, I remind him he must maintain his speed or get off to push his bike over and then climb back on.

SET PACE

The boys wander and ask questions. They want to go this way or that way. I remind them if we want to get to the park, we must continue. I stay at a steady running pace to keep us moving intentionally toward the goal.

STAY AWARE

We continue to ride through an area around baseball fields. Soon, we are on the road again. We stay to the right, and I remind the boys we need to stay together so other drivers can see us. I keep my eye peeled from the front to the back to make sure I am aware of all moving cars. The boys stay focused on their bike riding.

GUIDE AND HELP

The boys make it to their favorite part—the hill. Charlie, a bit smaller, struggles to keep balance and increase speed going uphill. I encourage him that he will continue to get stronger and stronger the more he practices. At this moment, I slide my hand on his back and give him just enough of a push to keep his speed and momentum up the hill.

ENCOURAGE

By the time we reach the park and play, someone will tell me they are tired or their legs hurt. I remind them that this is normal and that most people will feel the same way. We say together, "We are Dancer Boys. We are winners who never quit."

A NEW DIRECTION IS SET

I remind them that when we get home we will: have a popsicle, get a bath, eat dinner. I will tell them about anything else planned for later.

HOLD ACCOUNTABLE

We get home safe, ready for a drink of water. The boys put their bikes back in their assigned spots. If someone wants to toss the bike and head inside, I remind them that we have a place where we put our bikes and helmets.

SAFETY

Very few times during this trip am I in front—yet I led them the whole time.

I keep my eyes on them from the back. I let them develop their independence. But if they ever need me—if some animal is in our path, if we approach a shady character, or if we approach any danger at all—you better believe I will be up there instantly.

SET BOUNDARIES

My job is to lead and teach, set direction for them, and only step up front when I need to do something entirely out of their skill or ability. I also have to know the difference between exhaustion and the usual grumblings. There is a difference between "Daddy, I'm tired and don't want to ride back" and a kid who is sweating the whole time, or whose face is beet red. In the latter case, I'm tossing his bike and him into the stroller, and he's not riding back.

My job as a leader is to have them be so secure in their abilities and skills that they don't need me. I want them to be able to make this trip someday without me. Because of our times together over and over again, they will eventually have the ability to lead themselves or others the same way.

Leadership is not about accolades or pay raises. Leadership is not something to attain, but an act you display. It's about making the best decisions for your team. It's about others improving because they have been around you and trust you.

We all have a choice to lead. Will you take up the call?

FIND YOUR CORE CUSTOMER

Running a company is not a popularity contest. Your product or service will be a good fit for some people, and it won't be a good fit for others. It's actually when you don't try to be 'it' for everyone that you can dive deeper into your own niche.

Rather than try to be all things to all people, you can succeed by finding your core customers and building your business around them. As Simon Sinek reminds us in his TED Talk titled "Start with Why," the goal is not to sell to everyone; it's to sell to people who believe what you believe.

Consider Michigan-based furniture company, Herman Miller Inc. A more than century-old stalwart in high-end commercial furniture, it is at the forefront of timeless modern furniture design. Herman Miller specializes in products created by talented designers and sells to design-minded individuals or businesses, rather than through mainstream retailers.

From the start, Herman Miller built its business around its core customer. In the 1950s, Charles and Ray Eams, two of the company's most iconic designers, made a series of chairs with price tags approaching $800. Even today, most people would think someone would have to be crazy to pay that much for a chair, especially when they could buy a look-alike for $50 at any local Target. But Herman Miller doesn't make $50 chairs; they create iconic furniture pieces that shape design culture. They make chairs for people who appreciate the way they think—people who want a handcrafted piece of American history, people who value the best design. Buying Herman Miller says something about you as the consumer. Herman Miller lets you feel like a designer. It lets you be part of the brand.

Does Herman Miller wish to operate in every market out there? Of course not. But for their customers, they add tremendous value. Why? Because they operate and sell to their core market—not to everybody.

Find the right fit for your product. Find the client who is already looking for what you have to offer and then serve them at the highest level.

TOMORROW DOESN'T EXIST

One Saturday afternoon, my five-year-old son asked, "Is it tomorrow yet?" A short pause came over me as I thought about a five-year-old's perspective of time. As an adult, I sometimes wake up and forget what day it is. I wonder, *Do I have to work today? Is it a Saturday?* But then I regain some sort of consciousness and put together what's going on. I imagine a five-year-old might have this kind of confusion every day.

So, I replied with an answer I thought might help. "It's actually never tomorrow," I said. "It's always today."

That might sound like an obvious answer, but many of us live our lives waiting for tomorrow. The truth is that tomorrow only ever exists in our minds. The life we have is literally what is happening right this second. Like right now. Following me here?

Of course, we must strike a balance here. It does no good to say, "Well, if I'm not promised tomorrow, I'm not going to do anything today." We need big, future goals to motivate us today. But if we don't remember that today is all we have, we'll keep placing what is most important to us in the imagined land of tomorrow.

MOVING FORWARD BY FOCUSING ON THIS DAY

Poet Francis Gray wrote, "Today well lived makes every yesterday a dream of happiness and every tomorrow a vision of hope. Look well therefore to this day."

Take a moment to consider what you constantly put off until tomorrow. If the goal or dream means enough to you, consider how you will proactively make it part of your day today. If you can still only imagine a dream or goal in the future, perhaps it's time to stop wasting energy on it and instead focus on what you are actually doing now.

So, what are you doing now? Would you define your days as well lived? When you go to bed at night and ask, "What more could I have done to make the most of the day?" you want the answer to be "*Nothing.*" That answer doesn't mean everything about the day was perfect; it means you made the most of it.

HOW DO YOU RESPOND TODAY?

Sometimes it seems that everyone else is living the life we want. Call it jealousy, lust, or envy. We sometimes just find ourselves wanting what someone else has. *Oh, it must be nice to be getting that new house, wedding, cute kid, great job, or vacation with crystal blue water, tiki huts, and drinks with little umbrellas in them.* Left unchecked, we let this kind of thinking stop us from ever starting anything.

Let's imagine you start learning to play the guitar. It's fun and exciting. You fumble your way through, learning a bit at a time. You are making good progress, practicing regularly, and then...you find yourself at a Friday night concert watching someone two years younger just ripping on the guitar: moving without thinking, strumming any tune the crowd shouts out. Twenty minutes ago, you felt good about how you were moving along. Now, you can only think about what you lack. The next morning, when you find yourself at practice time, you have two paths:

1. You think, *What's the point? I'll never be that good. I have school. I have a family. I have responsibilities, I can't practice that much.* So instead of practicing the next day, you park the guitar in the closet. TODAY, you choose to pass on the practice.

OR

2. You realize how much joy a performance like that can bring to people. The experience inspires you to learn so you can do the same. So TODAY, you decide to look up the performer on YouTube and watch the performance over and over, learning how to move and perform. You also heard a chord last night that you have been working on and haven't quite perfected, so you spend the next hour practicing that chord until it feels natural and part of your normal movement.

That decision in your TODAY makes up your entire life. It's your own story, and you choose the direction of the path.

At the end of our life, we want to know we have done our best with what we were given and with the opportunities that came our way. We all have different paths in life. We all must choose our own way, given our unique set of gifts, abilities, and responsibilities.

So, what is a well-lived day *for you*? That day can be TODAY.

PART II

GROW

Grow focuses on growth and development. It's about being curious—about learning, adapting, and working toward becoming your best self because when you are at your best, everyone else around you also grows.

DOING CRAPPY WORK FEELS CRAPPY

When I was eighteen years old, I worked full-time in construction and started a side business called Shiner detailing cars in my hometown. The business was an eighteen-year-old's version of a lemonade stand—I made flyers and stuck them on people's cars when they were at church or shopping malls, made T-shirts, and told everyone I could about how great I could make their cars look. I started in my parents' backyard and then moved into a rented space in town. I was doing well and growing, but something didn't feel quite right.

Waxing a car requires a degree of artistic timing. You need to allow the wax to dry enough that it stays on, but not too long that you can't buff it off. If the wax gets too hard, it takes a lot of effort to get it off, and it ends up drying in a milky white film. On a white paint job, you can't see this straight on, only at a right angle. On darker color paint, however, it's very apparent.

In moments of weakness and the fleeting reward of finishing projects sooner, I would allow these blemishes to stay on white cars and trucks instead of doing my best work. I knew I could get away with it, and the younger version of me tended toward the easy way when he could.

One weekend, my cousin had me wax his big white semitruck. He liked that truck and wouldn't accept anything other than excellence. If he found an issue with my work, I knew he wouldn't be afraid to let me know. So, that day, I decided to do my best work. No cutting corners this time. I thought clearly through my timing and waxed and buffed each piece of the vehicle, one at a time. I did the door, then the fender, and then moved on to the bumper. I applied the wax, waited a minute, and buffed that section. I wouldn't move on until each piece was 100 percent.

The extra effort only added about a minute, and it didn't take that much more work than rushing through the whole thing. Best of all, when I finished, I could stand next to my work and be proud of it. This was a very different feeling than when I rushed a little and didn't do my best. I wanted all my work to feel this good.

CONSTANT STRESS OR CONTENTMENT

Doing crappy work causes a lot of stress. I always wondered, *Would customers notice my bad work? If they did, would they call it out? What excuse would I need to come up with to get out of it?*

Over time, I heaped shame, guilt, and nervousness onto myself. I ended up spending more energy hiding a sloppy job than doing it right the first time. You might understand this feeling. Whether from laziness, a 'shortage' of time, or simply not preparing well, you do less than you're capable of and end up feeling stressed out all the time.

When I was forced to show up and do my best, I realized how much better doing my best made me feel. Now, I constantly want to finish everything I do knowing I've done my best because I know *that* will lead to true contentment. In my leadership, I'm putting it all out there. I'm fighting complacency and the temptation to do less or get by with average. In turn, I feel at peace and don't have to question myself. Even though there is plenty of room for growth and development in my own life, I'm putting in my best right now.

LOSING MOMENTUM

If you decide to do sloppy work today and accept the outcome, guess what will happen when faced with a similar choice tomorrow? You'll take the path of least resistance, especially if you can 'get away with it' or you're not held to high expectations by someone else. Ultimately, you develop a habit of being unmotivated.

When you do your best, momentum builds. The momentum makes it easier to do great work on the same thing next time, and the momentum even flows into other areas of your life, making what used to seem impossible seem possible.

WHAT WILL IT COST YOU?

In every business, doing crappy work has its own consequences. What will it cost you?

Even when you do 'get away' with crappy work today, is it really worth it?

Hell on earth would be to meet the person you could have been. Break the cycle. Choose to do the best work you can—in this moment. Don't wish you could have done it differently. Start being who you want to be today. It's your choice.

FRIENDS, NOT MENTORS

Don't go looking for a mentor. Look to be a friend.

It's great to have friends, and I am fortunate to have lots of them. I have friends I grew up with; some I recently met. Some of my friends lead churches; others don't believe in God. Some have sold companies for millions; others never have any money. Some have young kids at home, and others are constantly traveling to exotic places in the world.

My life is best enhanced by having a wide variety of *friends*, not looking for a mentor. Why? Because a friendship is about mutual edification. No one in a friendship is the savior. There is no expectation of one for the other. Someone doesn't have to be the 'seeker' while the other one the 'wise counsel.' Friendship can be a back-and-forth. It's more give-give, rather than give-take.

Furthermore, you can have a highly practical conversation with a friend, whereas the same conversation with a mentor might remain purely theoretical. When my wife and I needed some advice on putting kids to bed every night, we just asked friends who were a few steps ahead of us. What routines worked for them when their kids were younger? What didn't work? We had an open conversation and immediately gained relevant advice. They shared, we shared, we all hoped for a bedtime routine with less crying and chaos.

THE DANGER OF PUTTING ALL YOUR FAITH IN ONE PERSON

For decades, Tony Robbins has helped improve people's lives by bringing out the best in them. He is credited with changing people's entire perspectives about life. Yet, he doesn't want to be your mentor. In fact, his Netflix special is titled, *I Am Not Your Guru*. He wants you to find what you need in yourself and to trust yourself and God, but no one else. He's there to help, but he's not there to be your everything.

The problem with the mentor-mentee relationship is often that mentees put all their faith in mentors. This creates a dangerous situation.

Robbins commands millions of dollars a year for personal coaching, but he will not take on the formal title of 'mentor' that carries a mantle of obligation. He wants to hand the responsibility to you.

You have to be accountable to yourself. Don't try to push your own self-discipline onto someone else. Some accountability buddy can't truly make changes in your life. Take ownership of your own life.

LEARNING FROM OTHERS

When faced with a difficult situation, make a phone call to someone you love, trust, and appreciate. If that person suggests something that changes your perspective, then you can make a new decision based upon this new perspective. But you should never betray your own self or deepest intuition simply to please someone else.

In my life right now, I regularly connect with one of my best friends, Cory, to talk about all sorts of things, from technical tricks in our industry to leading our families. Cory runs a company called Element 7 Concrete in Marble Falls, Texas. We met in 2012 as fellow speakers at an industry conference. We have met in person only twice since then (one of those times was a planned meeting at a Tony Robbins Business Mastery Conference). We stay connected by chatting on the phone several times a week.

Cory's business is larger in staff and revenue. He is also older than I am. I've learned a lot from him. It would be easy to call him a mentor. But that's not what he is; he's a friend. We challenge each other's thinking and provide back-and-forth input. We don't have formal calls or assigned times to meet. We serve each other and both benefit from the relationship.

BE A FRIEND

Zig Ziglar is well known for saying, "If you go out looking for friends, they'll be scarce, but if you go out to be a friend, you'll find that they are everywhere."

You don't have to wait on some sage to walk into your life to get started on your path. It rarely works out like we have been told in *The Karate Kid*.

If you want to surround yourself with people you can learn from, look to be a friend to someone you admire. Invest in their life. Listen to them. Support them. Only when you have given, when you have supported them, will you see the real rewards of friendship.

CHOOSE YOUR "YESES"

You make the decisions in your life. It's up to you to jump in or pass.

RESPONDING TO SOCIAL NORMS

Have you ever found yourself at a social event on a Friday night and wondered, *Why am I here? Why on earth did I say* yes *to this?* A week later, when a friend invites you to a similar outing, you wonder why you say *yes* again. What's going on here?

In many areas of our lives, we find ourselves doing things we don't particularly want to do. We want to please people; we want to be liked. If we're going to say *no*, we feel we need to come up with some lame excuse. But do we?

Entrepreneur and writer, Derek Sivers, argues that your *yes* shouldn't just be, "Okay, sure, I'll do it." It should always be a "Hell, yes!"[6] Sivers is reminding us that we are adults. We get to choose when to say *no*, and we can leave it at that. For the things we do say *yes* to, it should be a "Wow. That would be amazing! Absolutely." When we leave room in our lives by saying no to most things, we have the ability to do the things we are truly excited about.

Recently, my wife and I realized that Thanksgiving with the wider family had become more of a chore than a celebration. By the time we made food to bring, packed the car with kids, and drove an hour each way to our relatives' place, we felt we were working harder than we would on an actual workday. But what could we do? Could we really say *no* to the social norm of visiting family on Thanksgiving? What would our family think? What kind of example would we be setting for our boys?

We decided to break the norm and stay home. It wasn't easy, but I'm glad we did it. We stepped back and asked ourselves, "Is this really the best use of the day for us?" When we stayed home the first time, we loved it. Instead of being exhausted and crabby, we slept in, hung around, and watched a movie together. Our choice wasn't a popular one among the rest of the relatives, but that didn't

6   Sivers, Derek. *Anything You Want: 40 Lessons for a New Kind of Entrepreneur*. New York: Random House, 2011.

change our minds. In fact, we knew that if we kept going, we would only grow resentful toward ourselves and toward others. The resentment wasn't worth it for a "Sure, we'll do it." Instead, we set an example of valuing rest, being thankful for each other, and keeping it clean, simple, and intimate.

HOLIDAYS IN THE BUSINESS CONTEXT

Many small businesses try to follow the 'yes train.' Recently, I saw a man driving a truck advertising remodeling services. The side panels announced that he does kitchens, decks, roofs, additions, plumbing, and concrete work. Perhaps he is the most skilled craftsman that ever lived, but I wouldn't want the same person that's pouring my outdoor patio concrete to hook up my plumbing. By being a jack-of-all-trades, he won't have the time to fine-tune any single craft. You could choose to do everything, but is that really the path you want to take?

Jason Fried and David Heinemeier Hansson took this to heart with their Chicago, Illinois-based software company, 37signals. The company was already successful, selling many popular products, but their Basecamp project management software is what really took off. If they were to continue expanding their other products, they would need more people.

Fried and Hansson were not interested in increasing in-house head count to meet product demand and instead chose to go all-in for their main software, Basecamp. They renamed the company Basecamp, with a focused vision of what was best for them and end-users. By saying *yes* to Basecamp and *no* to their other offerings, resources and labor formerly stretched over many different products could now all be directed to further improving their software and making it more available. They focused on one core area and made themselves a more attractive option to customers.

Our company consistently has opportunities to take on clients doing work outside of our specialization, but we don't. By saying *no*, we don't overextend ourselves and instead pour all our resources and attention into being great at what we do. And every year, rather than do more and more, we try to increase our value by being even more specialized.

Sure, that means we'll have to keep saying *no*. It also means we get to keep saying, "Hell, yes!" By being intentional with our *yes* and our *no*, our team is trained to be great, not just good, and our clients get the best work we can do.

TOO OBSESSED WITH LEARNING?

Wisdom doesn't come from a conference; it comes from experience. Wisdom is knowledge in action. It's displayed by doing something with what you know.

On the surface, attending a conference seems like a good idea. But you need to consider the side effects. Conferences keep you away from actually doing your work.

I'm not saying that learning is useless. Learning is one of the greatest gifts we have. At the same time, we can become so addicted to all the possible forms of learning—reading, listening to podcasts, watching online seminars, and attending conferences—that we forget to practice what we learn. Knowledge is easily gained while wisdom takes time and practice.

So, what is your own 'conference'? What form of learning has actually become a distraction for you? Yes, keep learning in the ways that work best for you. But don't let learning become an excuse for escaping your work. Go to a conference, read books, sure. But recognize why you are doing it all. If you find yourself thinking, *This one will make all the difference* or *I need this to get ahead*, stop and ask if you are implementing what you already know.

After all, many learning opportunities already exist naturally in your life.

SEE WHAT'S RIGHT IN FRONT OF YOU

A few years ago, I heard about a civilian Navy Seal training center in San Diego. Regular folks could sign up to train like a Seal. I've always had an affinity for our military, especially the Special Forces with their ability to push so far physically and mentally. I planned to sign up, knowing the experience could make me stronger.

As I was gearing up to roar into this intense training, it hit me that my life was giving me the same opportunities to grow as I imagined the Seal training would. At the time, my three-year-old son didn't have a great bedtime routine. He fought going to bed and wanted to get up once he finally was in bed. Every night, my patience was tested.

In order to love my son and help him develop a good routine, I had to personally develop a strong mental fortitude to stay calm. One night, after he was finally asleep, I admitted to myself that I didn't have to travel to San Diego to learn discipline; my son was offering me plenty of opportunity to grow. Why was I thinking I needed to travel across the country to learn to keep my cool in tough circumstances when life was offering up the opportunity right where I was?

Every day, we can be tested and grow from our daily experiences. We only need to open our eyes to the opportunity right in front of us.

BUT WHAT ABOUT NETWORKING?

"Well, what about networking? I go to conferences for the networking."

Sure, there is some legitimacy to the concept of being in the right place at the right time to meet the right person. It's also true that many people neglect going deeper into the network they already have.

Furthermore, our current concept of 'networking' is silly. We've taken a natural process—meeting people and developing relationships—and forced it into a results-driven outing.

Anytime we take a natural process, like meeting people, and try to 'systematize' or force it to happen, what was natural starts to feel awkward. No, you're not nervous to meet people. You feel weird because it is weird. Listen to that inner voice every once in a while.

Rather than jumping at every opportunity, let intentionality guide your growth. Stay steady, and find the hidden cost associated with leaving work. Are you trying to escape your work, or are you planning a specific trip and training for a reason? Don't just be busy; be effective. Find the best ways and times to grow and learn so you can be at your best.

LET IT SIT

If you run a business, you are likely constantly hounded by e-mails, text messages, requests for decisions, and everyday work goals. If you don't prioritize time for yourself, that time will quickly be occupied by something else.

It's important to find your own space to turn off all of your distractions. You need your thinking time.

This time might happen in the morning before the day gets started. You might switch off everything for a while in the middle of each day. Or you might find that your mind is clearest when the rest of the family is asleep at night. Whatever the case, make a point of having time to turn off reactiveness and allow yourself space to sit with only your thoughts.

Most business culture today is infected with the idea that

we have to make impulsive, quick decisions in order to be successful. Many business owners think they need to run their companies like a reactive day trader. But the opposite is actually true. Sound and solid success takes time. Investment sage Warren Buffet knows this. He insists all of his company's decisions are long-term plays and shares his approach each year in annual shareholder letters. Before he makes decisions, he invests first in thinking time: he lets things sit.

Letting things sit is simply deciding to not make decisions right now. It's choosing to wait. Many people will bring you things that seem to require 'right now' decisions. It's your job to keep the path steady, and to allow time and space. Oftentimes, a single night of sleep helps orient us; it allows us the space to make the right decision.

So next time someone asks you to make a decision now, choose to pause, sleep on it, and call them tomorrow.

STOP DIGGING HOLES

We can find inspiration to reach our goals everywhere. "You can do it!" "Chase your dreams!" These statements can be found on Instagram or down the home furnishing isle at Target. I am prone to thinking about big goals, focusing on achievements, and regularly talking about discipline, consistency, and a positive attitude. But what about the things that pull us down? Where are the quotes like "Stop making bad choices today" or "Don't do that because it's got a three-year negative consequence"?

STOP DIGGING BY DOING NOTHING

We have all heard the key traits that make us winners. How about looking at the path the other way? What are the traits and decisions that pull us down?

We think about building a mountain to stand on, yet

our actions can be digging holes. Before any mountains get made, we need to stop digging the hole in the opposite direction.

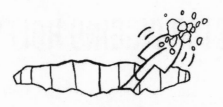

If you find yourself at the bottom of a hole, ask yourself what got you there. It probably wasn't a one-time event, but rather an escalation of many choices and habits that didn't positively serve you. Great, you've identified what got you there. What's next?

In Alcoholics Anonymous, the goal is to stop drinking. Not to get in shape, become a better spouse, or become a nicer person. Just quit drinking—that's it. It's one of the most single-focused organizations in existence. If you find yourself in AA, it's because alcohol has caused a problem in your life. But you don't have to do anything. You actually have to stop doing something. You have to stop digging the hole. You just have to stay sober for the day. That's it. Just don't drink that day—just one day.

But what happens if you decide to stay sober one day at a time? You stop digging that hole. Then you actually start coming out of the hole. Being sober one-day-at-a-time starts affecting other parts of your life. Maybe you start noticing you are nicer to your spouse. Then all of a sudden you feel better and have more energy. Those are the side effects of not drinking all the time. Those are the side effects of not digging a hole.

We all might have something that we are choosing to do that keeps us down. It's our choice. It's your choice. It's my choice. But before we get too excited about the big goals we have, we have to remember we can't reach the mountain by digging holes. We know we have the capacity for more, so let's stop digging.

CHOOSE TO STOP IN YOUR BUSINESS

All too often, I hear fellow business owners talk about being in a place they don't want to be. They say, "How did I get here, and what will it take to get out?" In business, it's easy to get caught up in things we shouldn't be doing. To get out, we have to go back to the first time we said, "I probably shouldn't be doing this" and then, find the courage to stop doing that thing today.

My wife, my friends, and my team would likely say I often want too much control. This isn't always bad, as I won't shy away from responsibilities. I'll put in the work to go towards excellence. But this tendency to want to control everything can keep others around me from their own freedom and growth.

I might say I want to work with independent people who make the best decisions for our company, but if I step in when I see any little issue, am I truly allowing them space to grow and learn?

Soon enough, I might have a team of people who are afraid to speak up, step up, or lead because of my jumping in. I wanted independent, strong people, but I could easily turn them into disgruntled, passive people because of my own control tendencies. This is my own version of digging a hole.

Instead of jumping in at every moment, trying to fix every small thing right now, what if I instead showed empathy and asked questions about how they are thinking about a job or how they might approach an issue. I could then coach them from there. In this way, I could help the future leaders of our business make decisions, while helping them understand the vision of the company we are creating. That's how I can stop digging holes.

When I practice what I preach—when I stop digging in this way—I can get above the ground and actually see what's around me. Now I can see those around me. Now I can see the future of our business. I'm not stuck underground, only able to see the dirt.

Remember, before we build we must stop digging. When we stop, we can truly see the fruit of our building.

THE RESISTANCE

Resistance is a test from the universe to ensure we are worthy, able, and strong enough to reach the goal. In the book, *The War of Art*, Steven Pressfield says, "Resistance cannot be seen, touched, heard, or smelled. But it can be felt. We experience it as an energy field radiating from work-in-potential. It's a repelling force. It's negative. Its aim is to shove away, distract us, prevent us from doing our work."[7]

Any positive force must have an accompanying negative charge; every hero needs his enemy. Anytime we set a course toward a noble future, we will be met with resistance. The job of resistance is to keep you from doing your work, from living your purpose, from doing your duty.

---

7   Pressfield, Steven. *The War of Art: Break Through the Blocks and Win Your Inner Creative Battles.* New York: Black Irish Books, 2002.

THE DIFFERENT FORMS

Resistance attempts to distract us from our work, stealing our attention through social norms, family and friends' expectations, and social media.

Resistance also wants you to label things because it knows you will waste a lot of energy on labels. It will say, "You can't do that. If you do that, you'll be a bad father, spouse, leader, follower, friend, son."

On the other hand, resistance wants you to minimize what you know you need to do to accomplish your goals. It will say, "You don't need to eat healthy today. You work hard. Go ahead and treat yourself and do a three-day juice cleanse later." Of course, that life in extremes will throw you off balance and rob your energy. Resistance again.

Sometimes, even people closest to us are, unknowingly, a form of resistance and keep us from our purpose. It's a red flag anytime someone says, "I just don't want to see you get hurt." Likely, that person is comfortable with who you are right now and doesn't want you to change; they don't want you to be more enlightened or improve in some aspect of your life. They might say, "I liked it when you did..." or "You used to be so..." Even if they say they want the best for you, they are holding you in place rather than encouraging you to keep moving on your path.

Resistance plays many dirty tricks. It thrives on drama, extremes, fear, trouble, victimhood, and procrastination. And the bolder the pursuit, the stronger resistance becomes.

HOW TO DEFEAT IT

Here's the thing: you can't escape resistance. You can, however, recognize it and name it. Then you can defeat it.

You defeat resistance by showing up and doing the work, day in and day out. Simply doing the work wins every time. The work beats resistance. You've got this.

BE YOURSELF

When I was in my early twenties, I got into mixed martial arts and joined a gym that featured mostly Brazilian Jujitsu and kickboxing. With limited experience, I had to learn everything in a very linear fashion. When I punched during training, I had to consciously think about my punches. I had to think about the placement of my elbow, which knuckle would hit, and keeping my arm straight. The goal in training is to develop a disciplined form and habits so that when you go to spar or fight, muscle memory takes over.

After some time, when you are hitting bags or mitts, you start to feel good. Within a short period, I was not consciously thinking, yet I could pull off combos—jab, straight, hook, front kick. It felt as natural as running. My moves were smoother, not as rigid as when I started. I was feeling confident, like I could take on anyone.

The thing is, the bag never hits back. You can throw punches, kicks, and combos all day, and you never get punched back. We did some light sparing in our facility, but as I prepared to do an amateur fight, my trainer and I traveled to another gym to do a more serious sparing session.

I felt good walking in, but when the match started, I found myself unprepared. I was in my head. I didn't know how to simply show up with my natural strengths and respond. When you're punching a bag or somebody's pads, you can focus on form and function. You can let your mind into the game and operate a bit slower. But in a real match, everything is much faster, and there's somebody hitting back.

As my opponent approached, I was consumed with maintaining form and delivering the ideal one, two, three combination. But that combo didn't make sense. I didn't respond to what was in front of me, and I got hit over and over again. My opponent had a lot more experience in live fights. The way he moved was part of who he was. He didn't have to think about every move. He could simply be himself.

GET OUT OF YOUR HEAD

In many areas of life, we tend to prepare for specific

moments like we're giving a speech. When we visit a client to present a bid or talk to a team member about a performance issue, we often approach the situation with a pre-qualified expectation of how it should go. In turn, we retreat from our true selves and strengths. We go into robot mode.

I've found that a better way to live life is to appreciate who I am in any given moment and not look for perfection. With this perspective, I know I'll make mistakes and say things I shouldn't say, but I'd rather show up as me, based on where I am right now. Craig Groeschel, founder and pastor of Life.Church, packaged this idea nicely with this quote: "Be yourself. People would rather follow a leader who is always real than one who is always right."

It takes tons of energy to be two separate people, and it never works well. You spend way too much time thinking about who you are in a particular moment, and you ultimately can't fool anyone. It won't take long for others to find out that the person you are at work is not the same person you are at home.

When you are yourself, you invite other people to show up as who they are, too. You remove the façade and allow people to just be people, not pretenders. It's when we give the world our true selves that we find the most joy in work and in life.

YOU CHOOSE THE RESPONSE

Stuff happens. You choose the response. Choose to LIVE.

This week we got hit with a few storms in our town. After a dry spell, this was welcome. We planted a garden and did some touch-up grass planting. Plus, I got a break from needing to water my yard each night. Yes!

The storms also scattered tree branches, leaves, and little fuzzy 'tree blooms' all over our yard. The time I saved from watering my yard this week will now be spent cleaning up my yard. Before I started to complain in my mind, I said: "Wait up Nick...this is what trees do."

I love the look of our neighborhood; it's about seventy years old, so the trees are big and mature. The trees sit near the road and span across the street. They create a beautiful canopy across the street. This look is what drew us to the home and neighborhood.

When storms come, the trees just do what big trees do: they make a mess. Buds and branches scatter everywhere. I can't control that, and I don't want to live somewhere without trees. It doesn't make sense to get frustrated because I have unplanned work to do. It doesn't make sense to fear the storms. The storms and trees aren't the real problem; the frustration and fear are.

CHOICES AND CONSEQUENCES

In our backyard is a playset for our boys—the kind with a slide, rock wall, and swings. They are rowdy boys, and I expect them to fall off or jump from the swing. In their pursuit of adventure, injury is bound to happen. Sooner or later, it'll be stiches or a broken arm. That's how it works.

Could I keep them safe, in their room, free from all dangers of the swing set? You bet I could, but that's a disservice to them and their growth. They need to play outside, to push each other every once in a while, and to jump off the swing a little bit too high, or decide to drop off the slide instead of actually slide down it. Dancer boys are going to be adventure-seekers. We are going to play all out, not take the safe path, and that will come with some 'setbacks.' But we choose adventure with risk over complacency and doing nothing.

Throughout our lives, we make all kinds of choices, and each one comes with a possible consequence.

- Choose to have kids, and you give up personal time. BUT—You learn to love in an entirely different way.
- Choose to build something, and it gets delayed and costs more than expected. BUT—You made something.
- Choose to go after big goals, and you get tested by difficulties. BUT—You develop persistence.
- Choose to trust someone, and they hurt you. BUT—You live free rather than in fear.

If you don't want any problems, then say nothing, do nothing, and be nothing. Of course, we should do the work to limit unnecessary consequences. If I never trim my trees, or I allow a dead tree to stay upright in my yard for years, and then it falls on my house during a storm, that's just negligence. That one is my fault.

But in the end, life is filled with so many things that you have no control over. Who says that the way things are unfolding is not all right? We think we are supposed to have control over everything; that it's all supposed to go our way. But it's not.

You can fight against it, you can try to control every situation that happens, or you can decide not to LIVE. You are stronger than you realize, and life and all its problems have worked out up to this moment for you. Why would you expect it won't work out again? Life's events will create situations that push you to your edge, with the purpose of removing what it blocked inside of you.

We choose how we respond to every event in our lives. The problems in our lives will either generate personal growth or create personal fears. Do you choose to let the fear build into anger and frustration, or do you choose to face and destroy the fear?

Choose to live. Choose to destroy the fear.

PART III

BUILD

Build is about building up the people around you. It's about leading others and creating alongside them.

SUCCESS NOW, NOT LATER

"If only I had a mountain home overlooking a river. That would be the life."

"If I could take a trip to a Caribbean island, I could really relax."

We all fall into the trap of 'if only' thinking. But if we take a step back, we realize what we're actually saying. We're essentially waiting for life to be better. Rather than 'wait,' what if we approach life for what it is 'right now'?

WHAT IS SUCCESS?

It would be fun to drive two hundred miles an hour on the Autobahn in a stealth black Ferrari. But I also know that I don't need to own anything or do anything extravagant in order to feel fulfilled. I need to work on my state of being, not on having or doing more.

If I define success a different way, I set a different foundation for a good life. A successful day for me looks like showing up and giving it my best, going home to spend some time with the kids, doing chores around the house, and finally watching an episode of *Parks and Recreation* and laughing with my wife.

Even in my business, I believe success goes deeper than reaching for a higher revenue number. It's about doing your best, making life better for someone else, and having some fun. If my staff and I don't pursue those basics, I feel we've missed the point of what it means to have a 'good business,' regardless of the stats we produce.

AN INVENTORY TO SEE FROM A NEW PERSPECTIVE

Take a moment to ask yourself the following questions:

- *Am I contributing in some way?* If today, you make a difference in someone else's life, you are living a successful life.
- *Am I having fun?* Having fun is the key to being and feeling successful. The truth is, if you're not having

fun in your work and relationships, you're probably not successful in those roles.

- *Do I need success to be happy, or am I already happy and believe success will come as a result?* (Hint: The most fulfilled people I know choose the latter.)
- *Do I make excuses?* It's easy to make excuses, typically because we simply don't want to find a way. A common excuse we all use is, "I just don't have enough time." (Spoiler alert: It's not about time. It's about priorities.) The truth is that we often have so many choices that we can't make up our minds: what show to watch, where to eat, which color shirt to wear—the list goes on. To stop making excuses, we have to prioritize and accept the choices we make.
- *Do I give my love?* We've all heard the saying that it is better to give than receive. If you're only a taker, you're going to be grumpy. Share the love.
- *Do I define success?* This is the ultimate question that will give you a new perspective about a good life and a good business. Don't let the world define your success. It's your choice how to pursue what is good and set your own course.

DON'T WAIT FOR IT

In his book *It's a New Earth*, Eckhart Tolle writes that success is not something you become; it's a state of being.

He says success in life is when the doing and the being are one right now.

Our business is successful today because we are doing and being in the moment. We still can have dreams of becoming better, and we can always learn and grow, but we won't wait for success until some predefined point. We accept our success right now.

Consider the questions above. How would you answer them when it comes to your life and business? What does success mean for you? Most importantly, can you recognize and enjoy your success right now? Why wait? Choose to focus on now.

MAKERS

Modern culture too often celebrates degrees, certifications, and the ability to recite a litany of information lodged in our brains. But what about things we make with our hands? What about that special value of creating, of making?

VALUE IN BUSINESS

I started my company because I developed a marketable skillset. People hired me to create for them. For me, it's always been a dream job because I love making things. I've worked other jobs in which I wasn't producing anything—where I couldn't see my work turn into something physical—and I was miserable. I need to see my work become something bigger than I am. I need to do work that will outlive me. I need to have a part in physically changing spaces.

Businesses in an industry like mine know they must create products for customers in order to survive. We take raw goods, create something, and customers pay us for the creation. Everything else that supports that work—bidding projects, accounting, maintaining equipment—only matters if we actually produce something.

AS THE BUSINESS GROWS

As our business grew and we hired more people, I learned the craft of developing people. I always dreamed of showing others the deep appreciation for making things, but that didn't mean I was ready to be done with the work. Still, people ask me, "Do you still do the work?" What they really want to know is if I've 'made it' far enough that I don't have to get dirty anymore. They see escaping the physical toil and sitting in an office rather than being covered in dust and epoxy residue as the ultimate goal.

No matter how many people I hire, I always want to do the work alongside them. I'm not trying to escape anything. In fact, if I get to work with the team for a difficult install, I see that as a privilege. I want to do the work. I also want to keep my skillset in check, and I don't want to lead from a distance. How can I lead well if I don't know what is really going on? How can I assess gaps in our installs unless I literally go onsite to see the work? How can I serve my team the best unless I, too, go and serve?

I believe our estimators and project leaders also must be able to work the craft. How can they sell, manage, or bid work if they have never been around the work? How can they accurately answer a client's question about our process if they haven't done it themselves? They can't genuinely communicate or relate to the team if they haven't been completely spent at the end of the day and covered in sweat and dirt.

If you're a business leader and a maker, remember that you're not in your business to collect accolades. You didn't hire a group of people to admire you from afar. You know you're called to make something and be part of something bigger than yourself.

Making is the ultimate way to serve. The work may seem 'simple' today, but we know we're creating things for future generations. We dream of the young child with a gleam in her eye, saying, "My grandparent helped make that."

EMBRACE THE SUCK

Go ahead. You deserve it.

I cringe every time I see that tagline attached to luxury brands or even local businesses.

Society has conditioned us to desire and look for comfort, and it's easy for any of us to say we deserve it. Yes, we all have obstacles to overcome; you are likely working through an issue right now that is taking your time and bringing stress to your day. That's how life works. But that doesn't mean we are worthy of an extravagant impulse buy or that we've earned a week off. Besides, a new (insert anything) is not going to help. They are empty fixes for hardships.

GROWTH THROUGH PAIN

What about a different approach, something more in line with the 'embrace the suck' mentality? Don't get me wrong; I'm not against comfort. I live in a temperature-controlled home, sleep on a pillow top mattress, and have all my basic needs met.

Comfort is great, but that doesn't mean we can ignore the reality of discomfort. In fact, if we embrace the suck, we'll realize that we grow through pain. My physical conditioning only improves when I train to exhaustion. My marriage becomes stronger when my wife and I experience difficulties together. Our business grows when we deal with and learn from painful events.

BEYOND FEAR

Our species has survived because our brains are wired to respond to things that scare us. But today, we're no longer dealing with saber-toothed tigers chasing us. While fear has its place and can sometimes be helpful, there's generally no reason to be fearful of everyday stuff.

I'm not saying we need to ignore our emotions. I'm saying we can see the bigger picture and recognize that discomfort in our lives is simply part of it all. Rather than looking for an escape, how about we embrace the suck?

THE RULE OF 100

As we move through our days, it's easy to feel that any single decision won't have much of an impact on our lives. We don't think much of skipping a daily run, ordering the burger platter at lunch instead of the salad bar, or watching just one more episode on Netflix. But the reality is, if we make too many of those kinds of decisions, we will start moving away from our true goals and passions.

When I'm in a rut or my life is moving in an undesirable direction, I try to identify where I'm going off the path by doing a mental exercise called 100x. It's simple but wildly effective. I look at a decision and ask, *What is the compound effect of doing this one hundred times?*

LIFE X 100

Every couple of weeks, the greasy deliciousness of a big

burger with a side of sweet potato fries is the perfect, feel-good solution for me. But what if I ate that meal one hundred times a year? Sure, it would taste great, but it would also put me in the fast lane to clogged arteries. And dropping fourteen bucks for lunch that many times wouldn't help my budget, either.

When I do this simple exercise, I see that the end result doesn't line up with where I want to be a year from now.

If I skip a workout, eat unhealthy food, or stay up late watching TV, I go right into the 100x exercise and take notice of what my life will look like if that choice becomes a new habit. With this at the front of my mind, I will, more often than not, pass on the comfort decision and play it smarter.

BUSINESS X 100

The 100x exercise can also be highly useful in business. For example, if Company A chooses to go the extra mile and take great care of their customers, and Company B chooses to ignore customer needs, they will experience profoundly different results one hundred times later.

When Company A plans one hundred quarterly meetings in the next twenty-five years to discuss higher level business goals, and Company B only talks about tomorrow's tasks, which one do you think will succeed?

You can also expand out the 100x concept in creative ways. For example, I look at finances from a 100x perspective once a month, so that I can move out of the day-to-day for a moment and consider the bigger picture.

I ask myself, *If someone gave me $100,000 to improve our company and provide a return on their investment in one hundred days, what would I do with that money?* That process helps me focus on what to work on to move in a positive direction. With 'an accountability' to a make-believe investor, how would I grow the company? Would I buy new equipment? Would I hire a salesperson? How would I streamline work at jobsites?

Take a moment to focus on one decision you're making in your business right now. Multiply that decision by one hundred, so you can see the big picture. Let that bigger picture inform the present.

WORK WITH WHAT YOU HAVE

Life hits from all angles, all the time. We must learn to adjust, adapt, and overcome. Work with what you have, and do what you can do.

If you allow yourself to tap into your creative power, you might be surprised just how well you can find a way out of difficult problems. You will be resourceful with what you have and come up with clever ways to move forward.

WHEN YOU'RE IN A TOUGH SPOT

In the early days of our business, I booked two jobs in the same week, both with tight schedules and each over an hour away. It was good to have work, but the problem was that I only had one work truck (which doubled as my personal vehicle). And John was my sole teammate.

He didn't have his license, and both jobs needed to be completed that week.

I made the decision to drive John to the jobsite farthest out in the early morning and leave him there to work each day. I then headed back to the other site and worked at that site alone or with another daily helper. Finally, I returned to John's site at the end of each day, helped him if I could, and then drove home. It was a beast of a week, with a lot of work and a lot of driving. It didn't make sense, but it worked.

We worked with what we had. We did what we could do.

YOU CAN, TOO

The human mind has a curious way of making things work. At first sign of a crisis or adversity, we think we need more time, more money, more equipment. And sometimes we do. But more often than not, we'll find a different way.

Adversity, in particular, has a way of forcing us to think creatively. Just ask an inmate who has spent considerable time on the inside. Prisoners have very limited resources and yet they find a way to make weapons from toothbrushes, bars of soap, book bindings, and scores of other objects. Some prisoners find creative ways to work out in their cells or learn something new. Their creativity is in full force, whatever they choose to do with it.

If you're in a tough spot, you'll figure things out. If you stop to realize that you have more resources than you thought, your confidence can be reawakened.

As a reminder, don't wait for perfect. If you wait for perfect, get comfortable because it will never come. If you want to be a photographer, for example, 'perfect' for you might be having enough money to buy a DSLR camera and getting a sweet paid client. But why not start with your iPhone and practice while you save up? Not only will you be more prepared in the long run, but you'll also be forced to be more creative with what you have along the way. Ultimately, your resourcefulness will pay off. You'll be able to use a better camera to do more than others can do because you've already learned to do a lot with a little.

Before thinking about why you can't in your life, ask, *How can I make it work with what I have right now?*

Work with what you've got. Do what you can do today.

CONSTANT CHANGE

The world around us is always in motion and, consequently, change is inevitable. Most of us don't like that reality, whether at work, at home, or in our relationships. But if we step back, we'll see the truth: it's not that we don't like change—it's that we don't like not having a say in the change around us.

My dad has worked most of his life in a General Motors factory, and the whole time, he never had a say in any changes the company made to his job duties, the work environment, or even his work schedule. Those decisions were made much higher up the ladder. The people leading in the company don't seem to communicate the reasons; they simply send a memo to staff and expect compliance.

It's a hierarchical, decisions at-the-top kind of company. Maybe there is a 'suggestion' box somewhere, but rarely does it feel like anyone's say or input is valuable. I'll assume that the higher-ups in GM want the best for their people and the product they create. Change itself isn't the problem; it's the communication (or lack of communication) around change that can cause friction. Today the company does it this way; tomorrow it's different.

This approach to change is common in most businesses; a decision is made, a memo is sent, and now there is a new way. But why? Why this way? Why the change?

Let's imagine I told my boys that I was going to pick them up from school on Monday, but something unexpected happened that day: I got stuck out of town in a job meeting, and that limited my ability to pick them up. Do I just say, "Sorry about your luck, guys. I can't pick you up anymore."

No. If I need to make a change, I need to put in the work to communicate with them. I need to say, "Hey guys, I'm sorry about today. I got stuck in a job meeting, and it was the best decision to stay. Dad needs to make that decision sometimes. Today, Mom will pick you up." By saying this, they understand the *why* for the change of plans.

The same principles apply for change in our business. If we make a change, we need to communicate the *why*, and we need to clearly share what we are doing now. Here are some examples of clear communication about change:

- "Hey team, I have always liked stocking the fridges with Red Bulls, but now that we are a larger company our Red Bull budget got expensive. We are going to stop stocking Red Bull, but we will continue to have bottled water available. Staying hydrated is a key to having a productive day."
- "Hey team, this year we are increasing our 'spend' for company health insurance. Our goal has always been to create a great place to work, and an awesome health insurance policy is important to us. This year, we will be covering spouses and children as part of our basic package."
- "Hey team, we recently found that one of the cutting wheels we use is more aggressive than the manufacturer led on. It works well, but we need to use this wheel at a lower grit level so we can produce the best finish for our clients."

For changes like this to be effective, they can't only be mentioned in a passing memo. They need to be communicated in several ways to stick and stay, just like a seedling needs to be watered and cared for to mature. You can't flip a switch and expect things to be different. Whenever you implement a change, give everyone reminders and continue to explain the *why* and *how* so that everyone understands the bigger picture.

You *will* need to make changes in your business and life.

Change is part of life. But you can communicate clearly about change with those around you so that everyone wins.

FIND YOUR RIGHT SIZE

Bigger isn't always better. I've made an intentional decision to not grow too quickly or too much. On the other hand, smaller isn't always better. A common misconception is that a big business can't do great work—that at a certain size companies stop caring and don't perform well—but that's not true either.

BIGGER OR SMALLER?

A company can certainly lose its way as it grows. We have all heard stories of companies just not caring anymore, or making decisions that seem to focus only on cost, regardless of how their growth affects the customer's experience.

Does that mean smaller is the way to go? We are seeing a powerful resurgence of small batch production, craft products, and farm-to-table movements. People often equate small company size with a better product and more care for customers. *Buy Local* is plastered all over billboards, bumper stickers, and TV commercials.

Whether local, national, small, or large, every business should find its ideal size and work from there.

FIND THE SWEET SPOT

Zappos is the world's leading online shoe retailer, yet calling their customer service number still leads to a real person who can help you. Their size hasn't hurt their performance. They've been able to grow while still maintaining their key characteristics.

Our company has a full-time staff of eighteen, which is a much better size for our clients than when we were a four-person company. When it was just me, two skilled craftsmen, and one person doing invoices, payroll, and marketing, we and our customers suffered. If a machine broke, I'd have to put entire bids on hold to fix the machine so we could operate the next day. Now, we return calls quicker, enter more accurate bids, and have more resources. If equipment breaks down, the team picks up a new machine while the shop leader makes repairs to the other one. Everyone wins. Project managers apply their full strengths to their particular jobs, and customers receive great service. We have the ability and resources to ebb and flow when we experience inevitable setbacks.

The key is to find your right size. Some businesses might be fine with one person doing everything, and others run well with one hundred people in action.

At Dancer Concrete Design, we're still in the process of finding our ideal size. I know that we need to grow a little to have a bit more flexibility and ability to get jobs done more quickly. Two more crews would help, but we don't want to grow so quickly that we lose our ability to care for each customer, and do our best work.

My best advice is to steer away from thinking that one size is best. Find the size that works best for your company and your business model. You'll find it at the ideal junction of being able to deliver your best work and have just the right amount of it.

NEXT TIME

In any organization, at any given time, someone is probably doing something that is not the best use of their time, or making a silly decision. We can't change that. By the time you find out about it, it's already happened. So, what do you do?

We can't change what has happened, but we can lead others to do better *next time.*

On the *Manager Tools Podcast*, the hosts Michael Auzenne and Mark Horstman often talk about effective leading. They explain that by focusing on problems in the past, you'll only bring out negative feelings in others that don't serve a purpose. Blaming someone doesn't help anything. Instead, the most effective strategy is to progress toward a goal together. It's all about figuring out how to do better *next time.*

I have experienced this principle in action when one of my sons wants to water the plants. Instead of saying, "Hey Charlie, last time you watered the plants, you spilled water all over the floor and ruined all the floors," I can shift to a *next time* approach and say, "Hey Charlie, next time we water the plants, can you make sure to keep all the water inside the pot? It's important because these wood floors can be ruined by water sitting on them."

Here's the simple breakdown of the next time approach:

- Recognize what went wrong or what didn't go as planned (without focusing on it).
- Focus on how to do it differently next time.

You know you are an effective leader when your feedback and direction allow others to make better decisions each time.

PRIORITY POINTS

There are certain parts of a day or a project that have more value than others. Not all parts of the day are equal. We need to find and identify the priority points.

A priority point is a point in time when your presence is more important than at any other time.

When we first started our business, we met at the shop around 7:00 a.m., loaded up for the day, and headed out. Some crews would get in a bit early and hit the road around 6:50; others hung out a bit longer and were out by 7:10. We 'passed by' each other and talked a bit about our jobs, but we were mostly in our own world. I was the main connecter, making sure one crew didn't have something the other needed, and generally trying to relay all information to each crew for their work that day.

That was the way things worked until we started a daily huddle. I took the daily huddle idea from Verne Harnish's book, *Mastering the Rockefeller Habits*, and these huddles have become a key priority point in our business.[8]

Now, we have a daily huddle that takes place at 7:07 every morning. The entire team comes together, and each individual team discusses the day ahead. We talk about what's planned for the day, goals to reach, and anything that might keep us from reaching those goals. Rather than being just accountable to 'the boss,' the whole team holds each other accountable. We also benefit from group intelligence. By sharing about each of our projects, each member of each team better understands how to approach the day. Each person sees the bigger picture of the company and not just their own work.

These daily huddles have served our business and have kept us from many problems. For example, Team 1 might say that their biggest challenge is the amount of work they must do that day. "It's going to be a late day for us," the team leader says. The team leader for Team 2 might then mention that their job is going pretty smooth and that he can give up a guy for the day to help out Team 1, or maybe even bring the whole team to Crew 1's jobsite to help in the afternoon. Or in another situation, Team 3

---

8   Harnish, Verne. *Mastering the Rockefeller Habits: What You Must Do to Increase the Value of Your Growing Firm.* New York: SelectBooks, 2006.

may be taking a special tool out for their project. When the shop leader hears this, he reminds them that the tool needs a new bearing, and he knows to replace it quickly before they take it out for the day.

If a priority point is important for a whole team (as in this case), everyone on the team needs to understand how important their presence is. Everyone needs to be there to share insights and solve problems together.

Some people say they don't have time for daily huddles or it's not conducive to their business. That's bunk. A daily huddle is a short, simple strategy that ultimately saves time and money through improved communication. For each minute we spend on a daily huddle, we hope to save an hour in our day. That seems like a good trade-off to me.

What are your priority points? There are not many better trades than one minute of communication for an hour of work. When you find these kinds of priority points, stick to them. They will be key drivers in your business and life.

PART IV

TRUTH

Truth is about caring for each other and believing in the best of each other. Truth and love are synonymous; love is the deepest truth we have and lies at the core of all timeless principles, including the notion that you should love others as you love yourself.

THE TASK IS NOT THE TRUTH

Lexy had already mentally checked into a yoga class. The two oldest boys were going with a friend for the afternoon, and I had said I would watch our youngest, Clyde. It had been weeks since she had been to yoga, due to the recent birth of Clyde, and she was ready to get back in a routine. Months prior to his birth, her yoga practice was also her 500-hour teacher training. She was learning so she could teach. Her practice of going to yoga had allowed her some alone time, some space to just be, to let go of expectations, and the opportunity to stretch and recognize that mind to body connection.

There was only one problem: she also wanted to finish her current house project—the refinishing and sanding of our home office desk. The desk, previously covered in paint, had started to expose a solid white oak. The new oak, once exposed, was showcasing mid-century modern features, looking like it would go perfectly back in our home when she finished. She had already put about two hours into sanding when she realized she'd have to stop to make her yoga class. She wanted to stay home to sand and finish the desk, but she also didn't want to lose out on her yoga time.

What would she do with this predicament of sorts?

TWO SOURCES TO THE SAME TRUTH

Let's put ourselves in Lexy's place. How might we see this not as a predicament but simply a choice?

The error we sometimes make is looking at each task by itself, rather than the truth it leads to. Both yoga and sanding a desk can be spiritual experiences; both can offer time to be in the moment; both offer the opportunity for movement. Two different paths; the same truth.

Beyond the activities, we get to the same truth. You might wonder, *How could it be?* On the surface, we see a quiet yoga room with incense burning. This looks very different than jamming to Ed Sheeran in the driveway, with a sander buzzing and dust flying everywhere.

But look a bit deeper. In each activity, we are looking to free our minds, let go of the to-do's, and just be with the activity in front of us: we are finding presence. Whether we are in a downward dog pose or running a palm sander along the face of a panel, we can find that we are in the NOW. We are there with the work. Our mind is right there with us, concentrated on the task.

Each of these tasks also offers a physical practice. The body is in movement. In our western world, filled with gyms and the 'shoulds' of life, we are told we should exercise. But do we have to do that in a class or travel somewhere to work out? The truth is our bodies are made to move, wherever they are. In the yoga class, we can follow the direction of the teacher and move in ways that align with energy flows through our body. If we're sanding, we will stand up, squat down, reach, push. It's physical work either way.

Both also offer the opportunity to know yourself. Both practices are going to present us problems, troubles, or obstacles to overcome. Are you up for the challenge, or are you going to excuse your way out? Yoga will present poses you have not mastered yet. What do you choose to do? Do you try the handstand even though you might fall and look silly, but you know this is the way to mastery, or do you bow out and just take the easy pose, so you don't have to face the struggle? Sanding is also going to present challenges. To make the desk look the best, you need to do three sanding passes, but when time is tight you might only want to do two. Will you even be able to tell the difference? What choice do you make? Are you going to choose the quicker or the better way?

TRUTH OVER TASK

We all get consumed with the path towards the truth. We believe the path we chose is the truth when the path is simply a journey to the truth. You might hear about Cross-Fit, do a little research, and decide it is the end-all, be-all for exercise. Or you might try a keto, Atkins, or no-carb diet, and fully believe one is the magical solution. The truth is that CrossFit or a particular diet are simply paths to the simple truths of moving your body and eating clean.

Yes, you need to choose a path, but don't mistake it for truth. Look to where it leads, and keep your focus there. A life defined by truths, rather than tasks, is a beautiful thing.

Whether Lexy chose to put away her tools and attend the yoga class or continue on her current path didn't make a difference. Whatever choice she made, as long as she made it based on the truth she was seeking, was the right choice for her. Sure, a certain path might be better for you in a given time, but the key is to keep your focus on the bigger truth you're after. If you do, you can be more flexible with the specific paths you choose to get there.

The truth is not a result of the path. Truth is always there.

FALLING IS OKAY

Life has a funny way of bringing us back to the poignant lessons we learned growing up.

I learned this truth up close when I became a dad. As a parent, you remember so many of the lessons you had to learn growing up. You are tested in patience and grow in love, but you also realize important truths about yourself. For me, being a parent is one of the most fulfilling parts of my life, and it has also helped shape my development as a business leader.

LEARNING TO RIDE WITHOUT TRAINING WHEELS

I don't know what particular event set the new tone. Maybe we saw another kid riding their bike freely with no support. Whatever the reason, we decided it was time for Clark to learn how to ride his bike with no training wheels.

Just a year and a half ago for his third birthday, he received his bike. At that time he was not even tall enough to fully pedal. His feet would come up short every time the pedal reached the bottom of the swing. Now, a year and a half later, this kid was riding up and down the sidewalk screaming and yelling with joy because of the new freedom of not using training wheels. But after taking a few falls and getting a few scrapes, he had lost his joy of riding and asked if we would put his training wheels back on.

As I saw this process unfold over two weeks, I realized how comparable this is to life. We all need to adjust or change as we travel along life's path. If we want to grow and improve—if we want more freedom in life—we have to be willing to pay the price.

Learning to ride without training wheels comes with some crashes, scratches, and bruises. During the process of learning to ride, a child naturally wants to go back to the training wheels. He wants to return to what was easier. He remembers how riding a bike used to be fun and full of joy. Now without the training wheels he's scared, and he doesn't like it.

Isn't this how change so often works in our lives? We want to make a change, we get excited, and we start moving forward. Then suddenly, it's uncomfortable. It gets hard.

It's taking too much time. We are doing the work and not seeing the results.

So what do we do? In a weak moment, we quit. We go back to the old way, the comfortable way. We put our training wheels back on and then we develop the excuse as to why it didn't work. We find a way to excuse ourselves from not moving forward. But there is another way.

Instead of 'giving in' to training wheels, Clark was up to working through his fear with me. We practiced takeoffs, pedaling strong, and stopping. He learned a whole new way to ride. He kept with it. I walked alongside him, and he slowly built confidence for two weeks. I held onto his seat while he peddled, then his shoulder. Finally, my hand was on his shirt, not offering any real support but letting him know I was close.

Then in one moment, I let go, ran alongside him, and he kept pedaling. He made it twenty feet and stopped. Alexis and I screamed, "YAY!! You did it. You just rode your bike all by yourself."

That was it. A smile grew across his face, and he was off. He had reached the tipping point of riding by himself. In one small, very memorable moment, our little boy was riding a bike.

TRANSLATING THE LESSON TO LIFE

Learning to ride without training wheels comes with crashes, bumps, and bruises. During the process, we tend to retreat to our safety nets. But when we see that falling is okay and that we can progressively reach our goals, something clicks. We gain confidence and ultimately, realize we can do something we couldn't do before.

My son reminded me that falling is normal, that growing and getting somewhere new in life requires a process. We need to be there for each other as we learn. We need to use the bumps to get stronger and ride on. Together, we can take off the training wheels.

THE CARING MINDSET

If you start to let things slide in your relationship with your spouse, your kids, your job, or your exercise, complacency creeps in.

COMPLACENCY, THE OPPOSITE OF CARE

As an organization grows, complacency can easily take hold and attack everything you stand for. If you want to build an amazing company that impacts people, it's vital you recognize complacency so you can fight against it. Yes, fight, because complacency is not some passive foe. It is attacking everything we stand for. A caring mindset is about caring about the things you do and the people around you. Complacency is a form of NOT caring.

For me, it's helpful to remember the early days of my company when I would stay up late into the night to get a bid to a new client. I ask myself: *Am I still willing to work hard to care about clients today like I did in the pursuit of building my business?* Of course, I now have better processes and a team that is in this with me, but the caring mindset should not change.

HAVE THE RIGHT MINDSET NOW AND LATER

Any time our business gets any press it seems that financial advisors and insurance folks are interested in talking about our current coverages and investments—touting how a quick review can offer us the best prices. These meetings take precious time. And although we want to get the best value for our dollars spent, I'm not about to switch carriers for a little bit of savings here or there. I value long-term relationships, and if I feel our current company has our best interest in mind, then we stick with them. That's why we kept the same insurance carrier for many years—until they grew complacent.

When the business started, our first insurance policy was an essential plan, covering the old van and a few tools. It included the necessary business umbrella. The total cost was sixty dollars per month.

Well, a bit has changed since then. Now we have multiple crews, six vehicles on the road, three large enclosed trailers full of capital equipment, and an insurance policy that protects us and our clients for some of the biggest construction projects in our region. You can do the math; we now have a pretty substantial premium difference.

As we grew, our insurance carrier told us they could not insure drivers under the age of 25. With 28 percent of our workforce under 25, this presented a problem. We send people out in trucks every day. Driving is a significant part of working with our team. This policy seemed silly to me, and after reaching out to some other providers, we found that this was a specific policy for our carrier, but not an insurance standard. So, I called our carrier and let them know the pain point for us, explaining that we needed to find some way around it to continue with them.

We were met with passivity. They kept beating around the topic, saying they couldn't change this standard. So, we met with other carriers. Yes, this was the time to finally meet with the people who had been knocking at our door. We shared our requirement, and they made sure we could insure any legal driver with limited infractions.

Once we selected a new company, I contacted our carrier and let them know we were switching. Now things were different. They said they could make an exception to our policy—that they would make phone calls to the underwriters to make it happen. They had the same opportunity as before, but complacency had moved in.

Instead of moving as they do for a new client, or when a client is pulling coverage, they were complacent. They went from "That's how it is" to "We can make it happen." But they were too late. They had already lost our business.

In your own business, do you care for existing clients just like you treat new ones? Similarly, do you treat your team members that have been with you five years the same as you treat new hires? A caring mindset doesn't waver in and out; it's a consistent mindset.

Don't let complacency take hold. Instead, care.

PAY ATTENTION TO THE PROCESS

Once or twice a week, I climb aboard an exercise rower. When I first started this practice, I was somewhat intimidated by the rower. I had seen people use them before, but I had never been on one. After learning the basics, I added the exercise to my weekly routine.

I typically use this rower for sets of 500-meter sprints. I go for a specific distance and then keep an eye on my time. I see my time per 500 meters, which is my pace.

The movement for a row includes extending your legs, pulling your arms towards your chest, and leaning back just a bit. On the way in, you extend your arms and pull your legs to your chest. You recoil to explode again, stretch your legs, and pull the handle towards your chest.

There is a process to do it right. If done wrong, you might open yourself to injury, and you also put in a lot of effort for minimal results.

Sometimes when rowing, my mind wanders a bit. I take my focus off the process, and I focus only on increasing my pace, watching the time as I row. Because I'm lost in thought, I don't maintain my form. I might move faster for a while, but it's not sustainable. Plus, I look like a fool because I have not dialed in my form and process enough yet to effectively pull at that speed.

I always get the best results when I focus on the process instead of the time. When I think about my pull form, get the best extensions and recoils, and am not thinking about the time, I not only pull faster overall, but the exercise is more effective.

The goal is achieved as a by-product of the right process.

This principle is true in business as well. We need a process to succeed. We need to maintain the right form in our operations. It may seem like we get ahead by letting process go (like pulling fast on the rower, but being sloppy), but this approach is short-lived and not sustainable or scalable. We will always find our best results when we are bringing focus and form to our work. Good processes serve us and provide consistent results. If you run a small business, you need to have processes in place to document your systems, or you will only continue to have a rushed, reactionary feeling in your work. Ensure that you learn from your past. Take time to build documentation, checklists, and reminders. It's a constant work in progress. We learn, we document processes, we train others to follow the processes. Then we learn again and repeat.

Don't take the shortcut that isn't sustainable or scalable. Stay focused. Build and maintain the right processes.

COMMUNICATION IS A SERVICE

With all communication, the key is to view it in conjunction with service. Are you actually serving the other person—whether a friend or client—by how you communicate? Is what you are about to say necessary? Is it kind? Is it true?

LACKING GOOD COMMUNICATION

We had a construction crew at our home, installing final base trim in the hall, bathroom, and bedroom. These guys do nice work, take their time with things, and stop and think before moving forward. But they seem to lack communication skills.

After they finished, I noticed the floors were not level.

I had never noticed before, but with new straight trim installed, there seemed to be a dip in our floor. I double-checked by putting a long straight board to the wall. Sure enough, there were noticeable gaps. When the crew left, the notion was, "We're all done. Everything looks good. Thanks for working with us." The trim install did look great, but the finished product was less than ideal. We wanted a clean, crisp line where the trim meets the floor, and now we had to solve this new issue: a gap under the trim and the floor.

I don't blame the contractor; the floor wasn't level, and that's on us. The problem was that the issue was never brought up. The crew could have talked with us about options up front, but they didn't bring anything to our attention. I would have understood there was an issue, that there would be additional costs, scheduling concerns, and more. But I was not presented with any options.

What made this situation more difficult was that it affected us personally. We couldn't move back into our bedroom. Although they said they were done, we had a new problem to solve. Before moving all the furniture back in, we'd need to fix the noticeable, uneven gap between the hard surface concrete floor and the wood base.

A BETTER WAY

What can we learn from the crew? How can you use this example to think of how to serve your customers through better communication? Here are four handy steps to good communication that create a positive outcome:

1. *Think beyond the work.* Your customers hire you to do work they can't or don't want to do. They also rely on you to know the big picture—not just know how to do the work.

2. *Recognize when something doesn't look right.* If there's an issue that will keep you from producing the best work or meeting a customer's expectations, don't ignore the issue. Come up with a solution.

3. *Talk to the customer.* Show them what's going on and share options on how to proceed. If it's a simple fix, take care of it. If it's more involved, discuss what is acceptable and plan next steps.

4. *Enjoy doing great work and take pride in it.* This is a final step, but also an overall principle. If you strive to do excellent work, good communication that serves the customer will follow.

If the crew had talked with me up front, and I'd been able to see more work was needed, I would have agreed to a higher proposal for that work and had them continue. Instead, this problem now fell in my hands.

Communicating makes the customer feel appreciated, and good communication doesn't require much extra effort. People don't want to be left in the dark, deceived, or forgotten about. By keeping communication kind, timely, and clear, you show others that you care.

33

MAKE IT A WIN/WIN

On Friday nights, our boys get to watch movies in their bedrooms. Their rooms are usually free of electronics, but on Fridays, after they brush their teeth and stumble into their pajamas, they have something to look forward to. In turn, Alexis and I are treated to a smooth bedtime routine and an hour and a half of quiet time. This is a win/win in our family.

I believe businesses can be run by the win/win principle as well. This principle implies that business transactions should never be win/lose scenarios. In his book, *The Master Key System*, Charles Haanel explains why. He argues that your win should never be at someone else's loss because that will ultimately come back and turn into a disadvantage for you. He writes, "The trained mind knows that every transaction must benefit every person who is in any way connected with the transaction. Any attempt to profit by the weakness, ignorance, or necessity of another will inevitably operate to his own disadvantage."

Haanel goes on to say that the individual is part of the universal. If one part antagonizes another part, that part will suffer, too. The welfare of each part depends on an interest in the whole.[9]

Sometimes people think that only they can win and everyone else must lose. Although this may be true in sports, I have yet to find it true in other parts of life. It's fun to work alongside people who want each other to win. We can't expect everyone to operate the same. What we can do though is listen, be patient, communicate well, prepare well, work hard, and know that all our work contributes to serving someone else.

When we serve clients and make it a WIN for them, it's a WIN for us.

Cheers to the WINS you create.

---

9   Haanel, Charles F. *The Master Key System*. Wilkes-Barre, PA: Kallisti Publishing, 2011.

MY TURN ON THE TRAIL

An off-the-radar trail follows the contours of the Saint Joe River near my home. The trail loops through the woods and over gently rolling hills. It's a secluded path that forks away from the paved and much more refined River Greenway, which connects the city's parks. I regularly use what I now refer to as 'my' trail to run, away from most of the crowds on the main pathway.

I love the adventure of trail running—a new log to hurdle or a leaning branch to duck under makes it more exciting. You need to pay attention and problem-solve the whole way to not trip over a rock or miss a turn.

The path is only about fifteen inches wide for most of its length, with encroaching foliage, muddy or washed-out sections, and giant spider webs blocking the way.

WITHOUT RECOGNITION

For the past five years, the path has been maintained by someone—a mysterious soul I've never seen. I always imagined a weathered, gray-haired hippie runner who became the self-appointed trail caretaker two decades ago, cleaning out brush and removing scattered debris. Sure, I've picked up a fallen branch or moved a log out of the way now and again, but overall, I've enjoyed the trail without having to do the work of clearing the impassable areas.

Recently, however, the maintenance stopped. Maybe that person moved away or just doesn't hike or run anymore. With such a quick change, I realized that all this time, I've only been a 'taker' on the trail, using it whenever I wanted while someone else took care of it. Left to its own devices, brush has moved in, and debris has piled up to the point that some areas are impassable. I can still weasel my way under, through, or over obstacles to get in a decent run, but it takes away from the experience. Due to the condition of the path, fewer people are able to discover this scenic run along the river. It doesn't look like an inviting trailhead.

MY TURN

So, I'm stepping up. There's no official title, and no one asked me to do this; I'm just going to take care of the trail.

In a world that is often afraid to step off the paved path, I'm not waiting for anyone else to make the first move. The trail is important to me. I want a curious family to go out on an adventure, find a new fishing spot along the river, get a little dirty, or climb a tree. I want other runners to enjoy the trail as much as I have.

Yes, I could simply take the easy way out and leave it alone, but in this water-rich environment with regular flooding and jungle-like foliage growth, the trail could disappear in a year. I'm not letting that happen—for me or the people I'll never meet who want to use the trail.

I will become that mysterious soul who cares for the trail.

STEP UP

In life and in business, you can't wait for permission to step up.

The business world is full of needs that don't fit neatly in specific job titles. In some cases, you'll need to be the one to meet those needs, even when you aren't recognized. By stepping up and taking your turn on the trail, you'll make it better for everyone.

LIFE TAKES TIME

Ordinary things done consistently over time produce the rewards we want.

Let's imagine your child celebrates Earth Day at school and comes home with something that looks like a leaf in a bag of soil. The tag says 'maple tree.' *Really, a maple tree,* you think, as you look outside at the huge fifty-year maple in your backyard. How can that come from that? You know that's how it starts, but having it in your hand gives real context.

Today, your child learned about trees, how they grow, and how to take care of them. His excitement overflows with the joy of having his own tree. You look at the instruction tag on the little shoot, and you head to the backyard to start. Together, you till the soil, plant the shoot, and water.

Every day, you come back and check on this little thing.

In its current state, it needs a lot of attention and care. It needs water, but not too much. If the yard were to flood, it would surely die. It needs sun, but if you have a week of scorching heat, the sun could take the life from it. It's so sensitive in this early state. To be sure of its health and growth, you have to look after it every day. But nothing really changes. It takes three weeks just for another shoot to grow out of the main stem. Someday, that new growth will be a huge strong branch that will be able to support many other branches, but that's hard to believe today because it looks so feeble.

Weeks, months, and years go by. That little tree has now grown tall; you don't need to care for it anymore. It has dug its own roots deep into nourishing soil. It could withstand a flood. It could withstand scorching temperatures all on its own. You think back on all the years watching the tree day-to-day, you realize it never seemed to change. Maybe a neighbor comments on how different it is now, but you couldn't see it from that perspective. Every day it looked the same as yesterday, but now it's a completely different tree.

What has happened? The tree has gained its own momentum, its own strength; it can work independently. As years and years go by, it continues to get stronger and stronger, until it becomes the huge maple it was meant to be.

THE REWARD DOWN THE ROAD

Momentum works the same way in all parts of your life. When your business is young, you have to pay close attention to everything. Still, every day seems the same. It's hard to see change because you are in it every day. The changes or improvements are so minor, it's hard to tell a difference.

A lot of voices in our culture say you should have the result now, without the delay. "Why wait?" they say. We are sold the end goal, the climax. Quick fixes abound, and waiting seems too 'old school.' The truth is that momentum can be boring; it requires patience. Each day, you'll wonder when things will get easier and when the rewards will come.

But then, in a moment of looking back, you see it. Maybe somebody mentions something about your progress, and you believe it.

We have all heard this reality, but overnight success truly does take decades of work behind the scenes.

READY FOR THE YEARS BEFORE YOU?

It's important that you recognize up front the aspects of your work that will not produce results for weeks, months, years, or even decades. In seeing this reality, you will be able to maintain a long-term view of success. Short-term gimmicks no longer lure you away; you choose to take a master's path.

In our business, we work today for work that will come into fruition years down the road. And we're okay with that. In fact, that's our plan. We work closely with designers and architects in design and construction phases. After an initial project meeting, that project might not go out for bid for another six months, and once it does get picked up, there is another gap of time before work begins. All told, we might need to wait two or three years from the time we first meet with a company to the time we start work, and we might need to wait another five-to-seven years for that company to become a consistent client or trusted resource.

In an interview with the Internet Association's CEO, Jeff Bezos said, "What you see as success for Amazon today was ten years in the making."[10] Many people reflexively think that if they had Amazon's resources, they could accomplish anything, but that's not how momentum works. The CEO of one of the world's most powerful companies understands this. Even at the speed at which Amazon moves, Bezos doesn't expect real results to show up until ten years down the road.

10 Beckerman, Michael. "Gala2017: Jeff Bezos Fireside Chat." YouTube video. Posted May, 5, 2017. https://youtube/LqL3tyCQ1yY.

If you can have a long-term mindset about rewards, you can have greater clarity and peace of mind right now. You can stop chasing results and instead pay attention to watering and protecting the seedling every day. A few years from now, you might be surprised by the strength of your own tree.

36

DON'T WAIT FOR PERFECT

I'm in the locker room, ready to get a great workout in.
My mind is already prepared to move fast and start with
my warm-up run, but I still need to change my clothes.

Only one problem. I dig deep into my bag, as a magician
digs to uncover hidden items, but I find nothing. I need
a pair of shorts, but I'm coming up short (pun intended).
No shorts, but I'm ready to go.

Here are my choices:

1. Workout in my underwear. I'm all in, but I'm at the
   gym, not my garage. Twenty-year-old Nick would
   have said yes, but I'm old enough to know this
   wouldn't be funny, just creepy...pass.
2. Drive to Target to buy a pair of shorts, drive back (at
   least 20 minutes)...No thanks.

3. Ask the gym for Lost and Found items (maybe gross but quick and effective). I'm in. I ask...nothing.
4. Skip a workout. I only do that in worst-case scenarios. This is just a pair of shorts.
5. Grab my epoxy pants in the car. My epoxy pants are an extra pair of pants I keep in my car for impromptu epoxy installs, covered in epoxy splatter. They are pretty stiff, but I can sweat in them. This is my move.

I look a little goofy. Squatting is awkward. I hear at least four comments about my pants. I don't care. I'm here to sweat, to wear myself out, and turn off my thinking mind. I get through my workout. That's it—I made it work. I didn't want to take more time; I had to let go of 'perfect' and just get it done.

Even when I pack my bag regularly, sometimes I forget. Still, I can make it work; I can improvise. I'm driven to produce, not make an excuse for why it can't or why it won't work.

I take the same approach in our business. Rarely will the stars align that everything goes perfectly. That's the fun part of leading. You plan well. You do your best to prepare. But when something happens, you adjust. You find out what you do have and what you can do.

In our business, we choose to figure it out. That's why

people want to work with us; we solve problems and offer solutions.

Don't wait for perfect. Find a way, and make it work.

PART V

THE WAY WE WORK

The Way We Work focuses on how we think at Dancer Concrete Design and offers some insight into the way we do things and why.

37

SIMPLE THINGS

As our business grows, I often consider who we are as a company and how to get new staff up to speed as quickly as possible. We hire most often for entry-level positions. We are not only bringing people into a new environment and culture, but we are also going to teach them a skill. We expect it will take two years for someone to get really good at what we do, technically; however, we still need them to catch on quickly to the foundational ways we operate.

To pass on what we believe in and how we conduct business, I recognized a few simple things that help us succeed. When everyone on the team follows these basics, we all benefit.

BE ACCOUNTABLE

We believe in being true to our word. We don't rely on other people to remind us of our responsibilities. We're accountable to each other by first being accountable to ourselves.

LEAVE IT BETTER

We believe in leaving things better than we found them. We don't leave a mess for others to clean up. We take ownership of the work we do and care for the space in which we do that work.

BEST WORK

We do the best work we possibly can in the moment. Every situation will bring variables and challenges. We do our best with what's in front of us right now, even when it sucks. We always choose impact over comfort.

OUR SUCCESS FORMULA

We work hard, smart, and long. We don't look for the easiest way, but the best and most enduring way. We show up when it's tough and stay consistent, day in and day out.

What are your basics that you want to do well?

DEFINE YOUR A-PLAYERS

People make an organization. Every business has team members that build the culture and set the course for success or failure.

To run a great organization, you want A-players by your side. A-players look different in every organization. In our business, we define an A-player as a person who *shows up every day, creates value, is motivated to improve, and can work towards mastery.* No matter how a company defines A-players, you always know when a team consists of A-players and when it doesn't.

SPOTTING A-PLAYERS

Your goal is to attract A-players whenever possible. Once you define A-players, you can better navigate interviews, hiring, coaching, and sometimes firing. While you can certainly 'coach up' B- and C-players, you can never allow anything less than A-player behavior. You must hold the team to the higher standard, or your culture will crumble.

This truth plays out between stallions and donkeys. If you introduce a donkey to a barn full of stallions, the donkey will realize it doesn't belong and try to find its way out of the barn. Or it will start acting like a stallion. If, however, you invite in more donkeys, the donkeys have no incentive to change. You don't want to be a donkey organization; if you are, you'll only attract more donkeys and keep stallions away.

You can see the distinct difference between these two types of organizations by observing fast food restaurants. Consider Chick-fil-A and the fictitious Burger Donald. Walk into any Chick-fil-A, and you find a fully staffed, fast-paced environment. They offer extras like bringing your food to your table, helping out with young children, and exuding polite behavior. Employees dress well, and management expects nothing less than the best from their teams.

Now imagine walking into Burger Donald. No one is at the counter to take your order. You stand there a while until someone comes from the back, but they don't greet you. They just stand there waiting for you to order something. The order is finally placed, but then the employee wanders about, chatting with other staff. To make matters worse, everyone seems to have their own idea of company dress code standards.

Which of these restaurants operates with more A-players? Which do you think will attract more A-players? You can extend these types of questions to any organization. For example, only the best of the best get into Google. If you have any doubts about your abilities or performance, you won't be hired there. That's for a reason; it's an A-player organization.

Let's look a bit more deeply at five traits that make an A-player at Dancer Concrete Design. You can start here as you 'build out' the right list for your own organization.

SHOW UP

Professionals show up and do what's required, even when they don't want to. They work with other people even when they don't like them. They work even when they don't have all the information. They don't make excuses; they show up and get to work.

FACE FEARS

Professionals face their fears. They don't run away or

hide. We're all afraid at times, but a professional says yes and confronts fear.

BE A CREATOR

The professional does not criticize others, and they have great respect for other creators. As Theodore Roosevelt stated, "It is not the critic who counts...The credit belongs to the man who is actually in the arena, whose face is marred by dust and sweat and blood." He is the victor. He is the creator.

READY TO IMPROVE

You can tell when you've been around a professional because they leave things better than they found them. They take ownership of their role in any environment, always ready to be better than they were before. As a result, they raise others around them to a higher level.

WORK TOWARD MASTERY

The secret to mastery is that there is no secret. You show up, give your best, and repeat. You practice, get a little bit better, and do it again. Every successful pursuit first involves mundane, small, insignificant tasks, and the master knows repeat action makes all the difference.

They do the work when no one notices. They continue when no one is looking.

Did Kobe Bryant get great at basketball for the two hours you saw him on TV, or was it the long hours of practice before the game when he was the only one on the court? When others stopped to save their energy, he kept practicing.

Masters can't be outworked.

WORTH THE TIME

As a leader, you want A-players on your team because they will help you build your business the best way. A helpful by-product is a better reputation.

Take some time to set the definition for an A-player in your company. Take time to attract the right people. Remember along the way that whatever you expect out of your people, you have to live. If you act like a donkey... well, you get where I'm going.

EXCELLENCE IN EVERYTHING

How you do something is how you do everything.

My simple trip to the trash can outside follows the same routine: open the lid, toss in the trash, close the lid, go back in the house. I want to accomplish the task and move on. One time, however, I noticed something on the ground, picked it up, and saw that it was the dryer exhaust vent. I had no idea it had fallen off, but the inside was caked with what looked like years of accumulated lint.

In a brief moment of vulnerability, my first thought was to simply put it back on. *No one ever sees the inside of that thing*, I thought. *I'll worry about cleaning it later.* But I couldn't do it; I couldn't turn away from the filth, so I fit my long-sleeve sweatshirt cuff over my hand and quickly wiped the inside of the vent. As I went to put it back on, I realized I had settled for another moment of mediocrity.

I had gotten most of the dust off in my quick wipe. Some might have called it 'good enough,' but it wasn't excellent.

DON'T SETTLE FOR GOOD ENOUGH

In my business and throughout my life, I never want to settle for 'good enough.' I don't want to just talk about pursuing excellence; I want to pursue it, even if that means fully cleaning the dryer vent.

So, I brought that vent to the garage and went after it with my sleeve again. But this time I also used my fingernails and a flat screwdriver until every trace of old, miserable dryer lint was gone. It was a menial, thirty-second task, but I put 100 percent into it.

Excellence will require more from you. It will usually require harder work with its share of frustrating moments. It's all too easy to let 'good enough' take over. You have to be excellent at each step along the way, not just the steps you enjoy more or come easiest.

INTENTIONALITY REQUIRED

The truth is that excellence will never be for the masses and never has been. Unfortunately, complacency and mediocrity are commonplace in our society because excellence requires intentionality. Unless influenced by a different force, your mind will drift to that place of thinking good enough is, well, good enough. And that makes excellence a rare commodity in our world.

It's easy to talk about excellence in life and in business, especially when you are goal-setting or envisioning your dreams. But what about when something delays you or frustrates you? What about when you wake up sick, when you're hungry, or when all your friends are doing something else? Then what? Are you willing to be tested by doing excellent work, even when you don't have to?

You get to choose excellence by how you live today, because how you do something is how you do everything. Everything you do can be done with excellence, but it's up to you.

LOVE THE SLUDGE

Sometimes the work sucks.

Some days are frustrating, some are boring, some are nothing but trouble. Some days you want to quit. But you don't—you keep showing up. You know that some days will be magic, too.

No path is free of the suck. The grass is only greener on the other side because there's a lot of planting, fertilizing, mowing, weeding, raking, watering, and waiting.

But you think there's a different way, that there's a trick to getting out of the sludge...there's not. All goals come with a certain amount of suck, and you learn to love it.

In my company's concrete polishing process, we do what's called a wet polish cut. Cutting concrete creates a thick clay-like mucky sludge of ground concrete powder, dust, and water. Any time we do 'wet cuts,' someone's job is sludge control. The job is to vacuum up the wet sludge from the polishing process and dispose of the debris. It's the dirtiest thing we do. Your hands get dried out and cracked, your feet end up wet, and you're covered in muck at the end of the day.

But sludge control has to be done in order to create beautiful floors. So you have a choice; you can complain, talk about how silly it is we do this, and say you don't get paid enough to do it. Or you can embrace the messiness and enjoy getting paid to play in the mud.

Every job and every unique role has sludge. Rather than run from it, give sludge a big hug and love it.

NO TAPE LEFT BEHIND

We use a lot of tape. Like a lot.

All our processes are a bit messy, and yet we need sharp lines and tight work in corners. We have a priority to protect our client's property. The trick is we tape everything. Taping seems easy, right? You just slap it on, and it's good?

Hold up.

Although taping can be easy to learn, doing it well requires a mindset of excellence. When working in a corner or a doorjamb, are we using a credit card to press into each crevice? Do we notice when our line is not straight? Do we peel back and straighten it out rather than accept good enough?

Excellent work reveals itself over time. After a week of

working on a project, you will easily notice what was worked with excellence and what was not.

The day the tape is removed is exciting for me. That's when we start to get a feeling of completeness and accomplishment. At the same time, it's also when we see the little itty-bitty pieces of tape that somehow remained—in those hard-to-reach places and inside corners.

Our job is to do our best work and remove all those itty-bitty pieces. This is another opportunity to add to our reputation or to hurt it. When we do a good job cleaning up the tape residue, people say, "They do the BEST work." If we don't, we can expect to hear, "They do a good job, but you have to watch them and make sure they clean up." I don't know about you, but I don't want us to require supervision. I can be led; I am open to feedback. But being supervised is for children and the incompetent.

So, when that fateful moment comes when you must decide if you should take the extra five minutes to take a razor blade to that pesky piece of blue tape or pass it by as 'good enough,' let out your warrior cry, grab a razor, and remember *No Tape Left Behind*.

THE PAPER TOWEL BANDIT

He has struck again. His impact seems inconsequential to some, while others allow a self-righteous anger to stir up as they mumble under their breath. When I see what has occurred, I sense bigger problems to come.

Imagine this with me: you're in the bathroom, have taken care of business, wash your hands, and go for the paper towels to dry off your hands. To your astonishment, there are no paper towels. Someone had the audacity to use the last one and not replace them.

The paper towel bandit has left their mark—the empty brown paper towel roll.

Maybe this person was thinking about something else, not even aware they used the last sheet. Or maybe after leaving the restroom, they had intentions to get a few more rolls from the back room until they were interrupted and completely forgot.

For a minute, let's imagine that someone, in a moment of weakness, thought, *It's not my job to replace the paper towels. The next person can take care of it, or someone will refill these.*

This final 'reason' is the one that causes me concern. You might think I'm making a big deal over nothing, but I think this 'small deal' is a sign of 'big deals.'

HAVING DISCIPLINE WITH MINOR TASKS

When we allow ourselves to do what is easier in the moment rather than making the right choice, we lose our discipline for the bigger things.

This is bigger than replacing paper towels when they run out. What exceptions might we be making in our lives about what will be taken care of? Where might we be holding back from doing the right thing in each situation? The thing is, we already know the right thing to do. The answers are already in us.

I think we can bring forth our best in the world when we set the next person up, think about others in addition to ourselves, and look for small ways to serve.

The small things are big things; it all starts with little things. It's always easier to fix minor habits than to let them build. Sometimes it's just a matter of replacing the paper towels when you don't feel like it.

THE FARM

Around my hometown, there were a lot of people who worked a regular job and farmed before and after work, or would use their vacations to plant in the spring and harvest in the fall.

Think about that. While you were taking Instagram selfies on a beach in Cancun, someone else took their vacation to sit on a tractor until nightfall.

With all this exposure to farms, I have always appreciated how farmers work. They have a unique mindset. I have tried to bring this mindset into my business over the years.

FARMER TOUGH

To be 'farmer tough' is to be intentional about what has to be done and remain focused on getting it done. Those who are farmer tough are humble at heart and strong in character. They accomplish a goal, nod their heads, and move on to the next thing. They don't need to tout their successes; they expect success as the reward of their hard work.

Even if you've never milked cows before school, baled hay, or worked way past sunset bringing in fall crops, you can still choose to be farmer tough. Even if you weren't raised in the country, you can still have this mindset toward your work.

FARM TIME

A day on the farm doesn't follow the clock. You start early and work. There's no set fifteen-minute break every day at 10:00 a.m. or set hour-long lunch. You don't work until a bell rings; you work until the job is done.

Our company recognizes certain time periods, but nothing is set in stone. We take breaks when we need to and eat lunch to keep our energy up. On average, we end the day at four or five o'clock. But sometimes a job ends early because everything flowed smoothly. Other days, we experience delays and don't quit until later.

We don't operate in a 9-5 mindset. We're on farm time.

It's not about working until quitting time—it's working until the job is done, or until we find a good stopping point.

It's farm time. Not clock time.

THE WORDS WE USE

A thought creates a word, and a word shapes an action. For these reasons, I believe it's very important to maintain a level of consciousness around the words we use.

I have a few words that I simply don't like to use or hear in our business: employee, busy, and cheap. We make the effort to avoid even typing those words in our internal communications and use other terms instead.

TEAM, NOT EMPLOYEES

Author and businessman Dave Ramsey talks about employees as people who show up but want to leave, or at least steal and cheat while they're there. It's not a positive portrayal of the working world, but unfortunately, Ramsey is pretty much spot on. The employee/boss dynamic doesn't lead to positive results.

In our company, I have chosen to build a team in which everyone is accountable to the whole. We are accountable to the person working next to us, and we are accountable to our customers. I am accountable to other leaders in the company, just as much as they are accountable to me.

We are a team, and we use words that reflect this reality.

FOCUSED, NOT BUSY

How often have you heard people say they're so busy today or they have such a busy schedule? To me, 'busy' means out of control. I don't want my business to ever be or seem out of control.

Sure, we have seasons with more work—our peak times—but I'd rather view us as focused than busy. We might not be able to do a particular project for a client because we're focused on another one, but we'll never say we're too busy.

We focus on outcomes, and we don't talk about our work as out of control.

AFFORDABLE, NOT CHEAP

For us, the word affordable will never relate to a lack of quality. Everyone in our company does great work. Yes, we sometimes offer a lower price point and process a project in a different way. But we never do work cheaply.

I encourage you to take a few moments to consider the words you use. What do those words convey about your team and to the world? Do you need to change some of the language you use?

PART VI

BUSINESS BASICS

Business Basics focuses on some of the basic elements of effectively running and growing a business.

RUN LEAN AND
THEN OPTIMIZE

I only had work boots and riding boots, but what I needed was a pair of running shoes.

It was 2008, and I was recovering from a broken ankle from a motorcycle accident. I wanted to get my ankle back up to its original strength.

Four months of wearing a therapeutic cast-like boot had left my right ankle dependent on it. I was still walking with a bit of a limp. The normal course of physical therapy was a bore, and I was looking for a bit more adventure.

Up until this injury, I was active on a concrete crew. I was lean and strong from pouring concrete and all sorts of physical activity. Sitting around in my house didn't feel right. My body was ready to move. My brain told me I needed some sort of physical exhaustion.

I decided to go on a run, but then realized I only had boots. Thankfully, my roommate had an extra pair of shoes he said I could use for my run. I laced them up and was off.

I knew the park was about a mile away, so I planned to run there and back. This was the first time I ever ran for the sake of running, and I found myself tired before long. My lungs went first. As I tried to catch my breath, my side started to hurt. Then I felt the pain in my ankle, and my shins started to ache. The 'run' was actually a mix of walking, hobbling, and wondering, *Why am I doing this?* By the time I got home, I was sweaty and felt kind of crappy. But I also felt kind of good.

A few days later, after that soreness had worn off, I had the same inkling to do it again. I figured I could walk a bit less and run a bit more, so I borrowed my friend's shoes and was off again.

THE CRAPPY SHOES

The shoes my roommate let me borrow were his 'crappy shoes.' He used them whenever he had to do work outside and knew they'd get dirty. They had been worn down and had no padding left. But none of that bothered me. I started to associate lacing those things up with my runs, and I liked them. They were a bit too big and not right for running, but I didn't know 'any different' at the time.

I kept using the shoes for about a year until I finally figured it was time to get some that actually fit. By this time, I had developed a routine of running two to three times a week. I now saw myself as a runner, so I decided to go to the specialty running store to get my new pair of shoes. This store sells shoes that aren't sold anywhere else. It's the kind of place where they will watch you run on a treadmill to see the way you run and 'match you up' with the right shoe based on the way your foot hits the ground. Yup, that place.

A salesman approached me as I entered and asked if I currently run. I said, "Yes, two to three times a week." At this, he asked about my current shoe style and brand I preferred. "Prefer? I don't know. I run in these. They are some four-year-old Reeboks I got from a friend."

I could see the surprise on his face. He said, "You run in those? That's a basketball shoe, not a running shoe."

I simply shrugged and replied, "They are my running shoes."

Then he asked, "Do you get blisters or shin splints? Do your feet hurt?"

"Oh, yeah," I said. While I thought that was just the price of running, he smiled because he knew something I didn't. He knew that the right pair of shoes would allow me to enjoy running more and take care of my feet.

WHAT MAKES A RUNNER?

I knew my shoes didn't make me. My habits made me. I was already a runner for the past year. I had shown up to run all year long. I showed up when it was hot, and I showed up when it was cold. Some runs were glorious, and many were no fun at all. By showing up, I had developed the most important practice—the ability to simply do the work.

Too often, we think we need all the 'right stuff' before we can do the work. Maybe you see a documentary about someone running a marathon, and it hits home. You think, *if they can do that, I can too.* So, the next day you eat a salad for breakfast and go to the running store on your lunch break. *I'm going to become a runner*, you think, *so I need running gear.* You want it all—the right shoes, the right shorts, some fanny pack to put your water bottle in, chewy gummies to bring with you, and some branded running hoodie.

Four hundred dollars later, you now declare you are a runner and tell all your friends you are training for a marathon. After work, you put on all your new stuff and are out the door, but at mile one your side hurts, your feet hurt, and you're out of breath. You find out this running thing kind of sucks. What do you do then? The gear didn't take away the suck. If it sucks with all this stuff, it will always suck. What do you do now?

SHOW UP FIRST

We live in a world, and a business climate, that focuses on 'complete optimization.' How can I use my time the best? How can I 'hack' my way to my best life? We want to put the least amount of effort in to get the max out.

I'm all for improving and aspiring to get better every day, but we must show up first. Why worry about what shoes are the best in the market for running if you are not showing up for the runs?

In his book *Atomic Habits*, James Clear states that habits are built by showing up. He explains that any habit must be established before it can be improved.[11] If you can't learn the basic skill of showing up, then you have little hope in mastering the finer details of any task. So, instead of trying to engineer the perfect habit from the start, you

---

11   Clear, James. *Atomic Habits: An Easy & Proven Way to Build Good Habits & Break Bad Ones.* New York: Avery Publishing, 2018.

can do it on a more consistent basis. Standardize before you try to optimize.

In the process of being consistent, you'll know how to use new resources to your advantage because you'll truly know the value of those resources. Today, I know my running shoes well. I have a pair for road running, and a separate pair for trails. I can feel the intricacies between shoes from running thousands of miles in them. I can feel how they grip, the spring, the weight. Once I standardized, I could learn to optimize with the right shoes.

Even if you don't have all the resources you want right now, simply start.

When I started my business, I didn't have all the right tools, but I showed up and figured it out as I went. You can, too. No matter your goal, show up, build the habit, and then optimize.

PEOPLE

Great people are the Holy Grail if you want to accomplish great work. If you're working to achieve things that could never be done alone, the right people can make great things happen.

Of course, people also happen to gossip, fight, make assumptions, act in their own best interest, forget, and are sometimes just lazy. People can be messy, and that's okay. It's par for the course. It's your job to lead well, to point toward a mission, and get everyone working together to produce the best work.

Working with people takes time. It takes time to hire, to lead well, and even to let some people go. If I believed the adage, "Hire slow, fire fast," I would have a team of zero. What about, "Give somebody a chance, and if they fail to perform, give it time. Coach, lead, let them try a new role, and generally give them one more chance. Then, and only then, fire."

Here's how we look at hiring and firing in our company.

HIRING

You have work to be done, not enough people to keep up with the work, and now it's time to bring another person on. The team is worn out and excited to share the workload with someone else.

WHAT DO YOU EXPECT?

Don't listen to those old grumpy people who say, "You just can't find good people" or "People just don't work like they used to." That's a bunch of bull. I have a whole team of good people who work hard. If that were true, how would anything get done?

Simply look around you. You'll see people shoveling dirt, picking up your trash, mowing yards, running our banks. The whole world is filled with good, knowledgeable, hardworking people. This is America. We love a challenge and a good day's work.

These trite sayings are just a cop out. Hiring the right people takes a lot of work, and a lot of small business owners don't want to deal with it. If you think some online job post or a 'Help Wanted' sign outside of your business is going to do the trick, well, you're essentially trying to play the lottery. I don't think hiring should be a gamble.

HARDER THAN GETTING INTO HARVARD

Note: 90 percent of the hiring we do is for entry-level jobs where we will be doing the training. If you are hiring for a job where someone is expected to have a certain skillset, our method may not exactly work for you, but some of this advice could still transfer.

When we hire, we first broadcast the job post to a wide net to generate some interest in the job. In about a week, we might get seventy resumes.

Out of those, forty will likely have some sort of background in a related industry. We will send them a message, thanking them for applying and asking why they were interested. We might ask if they had the chance to get on our website and see what we do.

Of those forty, twenty might respond. Once they respond, they automatically qualify for a phone interview. It's up to them to now e-mail someone on our team to set this up.

Of those twenty, eight will set up phone interviews.

Of those eight, five will follow through and do the phone interview.

Once they do a phone interview with someone on the team, I will get recommendations on who to meet.

I will then set up in-person interviews with four people.

Of those four, three might show up.

When I interview the three, I offer the opportunity to do a 'trial day' with our company. A trial day is exactly what it sounds like; it's a day to try out our company, and for us to get a feel for the person.

Every company sounds good during an interview, and a lot of people interview really well. But in a trial day, everyone gets a fuller picture. We have the person actually do some work with us, and the trial day is paid. We want them to see how everything actually works, not just how it works in theory.

A trial day also gives the team the chance to have a say in who we hire. Someone might shine bright with me, but be a bad fit when they are out of the interview. And the inverse can also be true. Some people are shy and awkward in an interview, but if you give them a tool, you'll see them come alive.

Trial days are one of the best hiring tools we have in our company. Every single person in our company has had to do one and knows exactly how someone else feels when they do theirs.

Of the three we bring on to do trial days, the team will give feedback on who they think might be the best fit. Then we offer that person the job.

Of course, it doesn't always work out just like that. In some cases, we'll do all that work and find no one, so we wait a week or two and start over.

But generally, that's the process. It requires effort and time. Yes, there are great people to hire, but you'll need to do the work to find them.

The people interested need to be willing to do the work, too. In our case, we start with seventy and end up with one. That's a 1.4 percent acceptance ratio. That's a lower acceptance ratio than Harvard.

FAMILY

In our business, family is also a huge component. We have two sets of brothers in our business, and we have brought on other family and friends.

Be the place that someone would recommend to the ones they love. It not only makes you feel good, but it's just good business.

SLOW IT DOWN

I believe hiring should be intentional. Some people think you should hire before the position is needed so you're ready to go. Others believe you should make do with what you have and not hire until it hurts.

There's no magic formula here, but you do want to stay clear of impulse hires. Most businesses experience brief times of extra work. In these times, you don't want to reflexively hire someone and then have to let them go when the work slows down. First, determine if the spike in business is just a hill to climb or the new normal. If the latter, then it's time to hire.

DEPARTURE

This business is my life's work; I don't expect it to be everyone else's. Still, I hope everyone who has worked with us is better for it and the experience made an impact in their lives. I want our company to 'pull out' the best from people and show them what they're really capable of. Others in our industry know that anyone with time at Dancer Concrete Design in their background is solid, with high standards, and a strong work ethic. But while this is a place to learn and grow, it may not be the place someone stays forever.

Most people will, at some point, leave and move on from your company. Very few people remain at a single job their entire career.

When it comes to firing, I have made mistakes. I have fired someone in a heated moment, and I have also waited too long. I have seen the same dynamic play out in other organizations as well.

It's a lot of work to let a team member go, and some business leaders simply don't want to deal with it. If you're running a small business and fire one person, that can significantly impact the team. Still, sometimes, you have to make that call because the team will suffer if the person stays.

There are two reasons a team member should be fired: they can't meet the standards of their role, or they're bringing down the culture of the company.

STANDARDS

When someone fails to meet the standards of their role, your first move should always be to coach. Here are a few examples of standards in our business. Some standards might be general for the company, and some might be specific to the role:

- General: We believe in being on time and showing up for work.
- General: We believe in completing bids for clients in 48 hours.
- Specific: You must be able to change the tooling and recognize scratch patterns in metal-bond scratching.

One of the most common issues in small businesses is that the owner has standards that change too often or are not documented. In order to coach others on your standards, you have to be clear about what those are.

When someone routinely misses a standard, your job is to help them understand the standard. Make sure they understand their responsibility.

Coaching team members on standards is black and white. It's easy to gauge whether or not improvements are being made.

In some cases, you might find that someone might not meet the standards of a role, but is still a good cultural fit. In those cases, you'll want to see if they could work well in a different role. But what about when someone is not a good cultural fit?

CULTURE

Thinking through how someone affects your culture is tricky. You want a diverse culture; you want people who think differently, who had unique upbringings and bring unique perspectives and personalities. But you also have to take note when someone is bringing the entire culture of the company down.

Let's say you have an all-star team leader, Nate. Around you, he is attentive and performs well. He works hard, and his jobs are done with a high level of detail. You're surprised when other team members start asking to not work with him, to be put on another team. You know Nate can push people and you think he might be going too hard on the guys, so you ask him to calm down a bit. But a couple of weeks later a team member calls you and tells you all the stuff Nate does on the jobsite, how he talks negatively about all the other team members, and how he talks about you, too.

Maybe you saw a hint of Nate's negativity here or there, but it didn't seem that serious. You let the team member know you will check into it. The next day you grab a few trusted people and ask them individually what's it like to work with Nate at a jobsite.

The truth comes out. Nate plays one role at the shop around you, but once on a jobsite, he turns into someone else. He tears people down, makes people feel stupid, and does not support a culture of growth and positivity.

So now what? In your last performance review, you gave Nate glowing reviews. You even thought he might serve in a top leadership position. But now this?

This kind of situation can happen in any company; you might have a Nate right now.

He's performing, and it looks like he's doing a good job. But he's a threat to your culture. A threat to the business you want to build.

You might think that the choice is simple: fire Nate. But letting someone go should be taken seriously. The choice might not devastate your business, but it could greatly affect a person's life. The person should not be surprised if it happens. They should have early warning that their behavior is inconsistent with the culture.

Here's what I did with my Nate:

I first got together with Nate and let him know what I heard. I listened to what he had to say. We decided to work together to help him with some of his judgmental behavior. He knew it wasn't right and wanted to fix it. We agreed to get together every thirty days, and we hired him a coach to work through some of the negativity issues.

We put the plan into action. We got together every thirty days. Nate did the work with the coach, and it seemed he was putting in the work to make it better. Or so I thought. Nate said the right things to me, and at first the team even saw improvements, but in a short time things went back to the same as they were before.

When it got to the point that I didn't want to put a new guy with Nate, fearing he would skew this person's view of the company, I realized he needed to go. After trying everything I could for six months, I had to choose our culture. I chose to make a better business for everyone.

It was a tough fire. Not only was it hard for me to let him go, but now we were in a crunch with the loss. Still, it was worth it. It needed to be done.

But I also want to note that I didn't fire my Nate impulsively. I worked with him. I invested my own time, and I spent our company's money to coach him. Firing was not my first go-to action. I don't think it ever should be.

Leading in business is tough. It takes courage, and sometimes you might be responsible for ending someone's employment. If you remember that your decision is for the betterment of the company, you can do it with grace and strength.

KNOW YOUR NUMBERS

"I just pay an accountant to handle that, and when they tell me what taxes I owe, I pay them."

I've heard statements like this from so many business owners, and every time I inwardly shudder from their ignorance. As a small business owner, you must take ownership of finances. You have to know your numbers—all of them, including total sales, cost of goods, gross profit, expenses, and net profit. You don't need to be in charge of matching every transaction and recording accounting entries, but you should have a strong grasp of the overall picture.

AS YOU GROW

In our company's early years, I handled financials out of necessity, running payroll and balancing transactions every Saturday. I took a few college accounting courses and thought I could whiz right through, but I realized that real-life finances are an entirely different ball game.

Initially, we ran a simple accounting and payroll process, with end-of-year submittal to an accountant to handle taxes. One year, we finally hired an assistant named Dennis to help with these tasks, and it freed me up to focus on other areas of the business.

Every business needs a Dennis—the kind of person who is very detail-oriented and conscious of the money we spend. You'll be thankful for your Dennis. Believe me.

BE READY

All was well until we had a record year, which came with a record tax bill. Sales were great, expenses in check, and margin was good, but with no quarterly tax payments, I was in for a shock. I owed a big chunk of money and didn't have it. Where did it all go?

At the time, our accountant, Shannon, happened to be reading *Profit First* by Mike Michalowicz. In the book, Michalowicz tells of his efforts starting several companies and making a profit, but not always having cash in the accounts.[12] He dove deep into his business models

---

12   Michalowicz, Mike. *Profit First: Transform Your Business from a Cash-Eating Monster to a Money-Making Machine*. New York: Portfolio Penguin, 2017.

to create a simple solution: Pay yourself first: cut out of the profit from the company at the beginning, and learn how to run your business with the rest.

He gives the example of getting down to the last little bit of toothpaste and not having any more in the bathroom closet. What do you do? You start at the back of the tube, lay it flat and start to roll it up, so you can get every little bit of toothpaste to the end. What seemed like an empty tube now lasts you for three more days.

What if you ran your business finances like that, without waiting until all seems lost? You have a discipline in your finances to make the most of what you have every day. That's what the profit first system is all about.

Michalowicz's simple philosophy ultimately helped us pay down our tax bill and create a savings account with a strategic eye. We transfer money every week from our main checking account into other accounts for equipment purchase, charitable giving, taxes, profit, and team development. Then we have an account to pay those expenses from. We can host a party for our team, cut a check for a non-profit we believe in, or send staff away for a training event, all the while feeling good about the money we spend, because it's been set aside for that specific purpose.

Michalowicz goes into great detail, but his general idea is

that every time you take in revenue, you should make it a point to set transfers to other accounts, and pay yourself first before money leaves the company.

Even small transfers of, say, 2 percent of sales, compounded regularly, builds quickly. Financial metrics are unique to each business, of course, and additional revenue forecasting will likely be needed. But the key to running a solid, profitable business is to understand the big picture and prepare accordingly.

To have a strong savings account, pay yourself a living wage, and have money set aside for taxes, you need a system and process for your finances. A system like profit first has helped us navigate the highs and lows in our accounts, ultimately bringing stability to our finances.

DON'TS

Don't be ashamed or embarrassed if the numbers aspect is tough to understand. You're not alone; most small business owners are great at what they do and not great at finances. But as your company grows, at some point you need to come to terms with numbers. Don't let a friend or colleague try to run your company with his or her financial advice. It's your business; you need to know how the money works in your business.

For additional reading, check out:

- *Simple Numbers, Straight Talk, Big Profits!* by Greg Crabtree
- *The Ultimate Blueprint for an Insanely Successful Business* by Keith Cunningham
- *The Total Money Makeover* by Dave Ramsey
- *Profit First* by Mike Michalowicz

ASSISTANT STORE MANAGER, NICK

Thinking of it now, it seems like a different life—the two years I served as an assistant manager in a Target store.

Each Target store does tens of millions of dollars in business and is structured in a similar way. A general manager looks after the store as a whole, the executive team leaders play various operations roles, and a handful of assistant managers run the store from there. In my time there, I saw a lot of different leadership styles and personalities, and I saw how people handled themselves in their roles and with our customers.

Thanks to the competitive spirit of retailers trying to offer easy and convenient shopping experiences, returning merchandise is much easier than it was ten years ago.

Return processes today are very gracious and for the most part, customers can return almost anything without an accompanying receipt or even a reason. Returning items used to be frustrating at best and outright unsuccessful at worst.

While I worked in the stores, if a customer didn't agree with the decision of a returns clerk, the customer asked to speak directly with a manager, and that's when I noticed the biggest differences in leadership. When it was my turn to handle return desk complaints, I got kind of nervous. This was a first-time leadership position, and I wanted to do well. I wanted to 'prove myself.' Each time, I knew the guest would again have to present their return reason and why they didn't meet the qualifications of a normal return. It was up to me to make the decision for what to do next; I was the manager the customer asked for.

Back then I was much more prone to lean on company policy and *tell* customers the rules rather than *listen* to their concerns. I handled most transactions in a very reactionary way, like it would make or break my career. Often, I didn't approve the return, leaving guests frustrated and upset with me and the brand. In my mind, they were cheating the system, and I was protecting my employer, Target.

However, the general managers handled things differently than I did. I worked in three local stores, and I noticed across the board that general managers at each location approached delicate situations from a neutral place, understanding first and foremost that the issue was very important to the guest. Whatever the outcome, they knew customers would share their experience with others, so the managers treated each instance with finesse.

Each time, the manager listened to the guest share their story and almost always accepted the return to maintain positive guest relations. The manager might even breach a store policy to make this happen, and then remind the guest of the rules to keep in mind for next time. In the end, the general manager kept a bigger picture view when it came to returns. Other than in cases of blatant theft or fraudulent return, the general manager would simply process the return and go back to their other duties leading the store.

The general managers were not out to prove themselves. They knew that regional managers were looking at overall store performance, so they kept returns simple and focused on other higher-leverage activities.

In my business today, I sometimes must guard against being too reactionary at small things—being too protective of policy and trying to prove myself, thereby not actually listening to or caring for our clients or team.

I have to remember that I have nothing to prove. When I find myself being too defensive or reactionary, I ask what kind of leader I want to be today and ten years from now. I then make decisions from that point of view.

With the big picture in mind, I realize it's better to let some things go rather than fight everything.

DON'T BE 'THAT' GUY

Imagine that you just had a great experience at a restaurant. The food was good, and the server was excellent. Everything seemed to go so well. Then your bill comes, and you take a quick look. *Yup, that looks good. The appetizer, and dessert...wait, what the heck? A $0.40 charge for 'extra dressing.'* You just paid $16 for a salad with chicken, and they charged you an extra $0.40 because you asked for extra dressing?

Or consider the case of impulsively signing up for some online subscription. Maybe you used it for a month and forgot about it. Now a year has passed, and you remember that you're going to be charged again. So you fumble around, trying to find the password for the account. Finally, you login, only to have to navigate the whole site, up and down, to find that hidden link to cancel your membership.

In both cases, it seems the companies are looking out for themselves, rather than the customer. I don't know about you, but I want to be able to get as many sauces or dressings as I want at a restaurant. And I don't want to have to spend all day to cancel a subscription.

It's not about the forty cents. It's not about the need to cancel. It's that we all want to feel valued as customers.

WORK WITH CUSTOMERS

We want our clients to know that when they work with us, we're going to take care of them. If they need something moved after we get on site, we can help with that. If minor patching is needed on the floor that's not in the budget, we'll take care of it.

With this approach, customers know you care about them and find it pleasant to work with you.

SETTING BOUNDARIES

Naturally, if we start a project and find we need a full day to move stuff out of the way before starting, the old concrete is in worse shape than the client thought, or they decide to add another room, we'll need to draw up a change order for a scope of work change.

We set boundaries, but we don't have a hard and fast rule about extras. Our teams use their intelligence and experience to determine what we need to complete the work.

In the end, you want people to know you value them as customers. You take care of the small things. You make it easy to do business with you. You care.

IF YOU'RE GOOD, OTHERS WILL WANT TO BE LIKE YOU

Whenever you're in front, others want to be there, too, and they will follow you.

This happens if you're the fastest runner in school or the market-leading business innovator. Many people are afraid of the leading position. They fear others might copy everything they did or outright steal their ideas. But it's pointless to worry about these kinds of things. If you're already a step ahead, there's no need to be concerned about everybody else. You're exactly where you want to be.

As a leader, you have to prepare to do more work than others are willing to do. You might have to put in one hundred hours to create something, when someone else might copy it and make it in ten. I recognize that some people have blatantly stolen our ideas, but I don't put energy into fighting that reality. I have yet to find a copyright infringement in our industry that's worth pursuing, and pursuing it would only take our focus off of doing great work.

Don't forget that others miss out on the ninety hours of creative innovation that brought you to another level. By the time a wanna-be company copies your idea and does anything with it, you will have already started the next phase of the upgrade.

If you're good, you simply have to accept the fact that others will rip off of you. And some customers will even choose to buy from a company selling B-grade copies of your work. But that's not your core client anyway. Keep focusing on being the business that everyone else talks about. We like it if competitors say about us, "We'll do what they do, but cheaper." For us, that statement simply confirms our place as the market leader. And the right customers will find their way to us.

BE THE BETTER BUSINESS

In the book *The Fish That Ate the Whale*, we are introduced to Sam Zemurray. Sam is a young, scrappy man looking for a way to make money. Bananas are just being introduced into America through the port of New Orleans, and the major distributor, United Fruit Company, is bringing them into America for the first time.

Given the speed of transportation at the time, bananas would have to be very green to make the trip from New Orleans to the northern states. United Fruit would offload their 'ripes' that were too bruised or too mature to make the trip. Sam was one of the people who would purchase these ripes.

Sam sold these bananas and continued to invest his profits and grow the business until, years later, he could purchase his own piece of land in Honduras and his own fleet of boats.

Soon enough, the man who started selling the ripes of United Fruit became their main competitor.

United Fruit was a massive company with many high-level executives. Headquartered in New York, the people making all the decisions were thousands of miles away from the real work—the banana fields, the boats, and the ports.

In the short term, it seemed like the giant company would win because they had all the resources; they had deeper pockets and access to the best consultants. But Sam was intimately involved with the process and knew everything about the product. He was IN the business.

Sam didn't work from an office. He spent his time in the field in Honduras, riding on the boats, and among the people doing the work and buying the product. He developed a solid reputation and rewarding relationships with the people who made the business work.

After years of battling against United Fruit, the large company ended up buying Sam's business and naming him CEO. The little fish ended up being in charge of the whale.

THE PATH TO WINNING

I always enjoy reading this inspirational story because it reminds me to focus on being the better business, not the biggest one. Sam Zemurray was in his business. He didn't have the biggest company, but he had a drive to be the best in what he did.

Your customers, and your team, want you to be the better business. When you look out for others' best interest, they want you to win. When you continue to make the product or service better, it's hard to lose. You're on the path to winning.

Success doesn't mean you get to sit somewhere, away from the work. Your job is to go deeper into the work, to help make your processes easier and smoother for your customers and your team. The best business is the one where the leader is continually involved. They are 'building people,' making better products, and always looking to improve.

You don't win with a 'set and forget it' approach. Do the work every day, and see what happens.

Day in. Day out. Show up.

FINAL NOTE

I have a routine of writing every Saturday morning. My writing goes into a company e-mail with updates on what's happening in our business, things such as anniversaries and what projects we are working on. In one section of the e-mail, I share a story or principle I think will help shape our company. Most of this book is a collection of these. As time went on, people on my team or others who get my weekly e-mail would share how something I shared helped them. The purpose of this book was to hopefully help someone better their life by reading it.

Many people have helped me in my life. There are so many people to thank, and I don't want to miss one. I am grateful to everyone who has played a part in my life, and who helped make this book possible. So many people worked to make it happen. That's not true only of this book, but for everything in my life.

I believe God has a purpose for my life, and for me. This book is part of it. But it's not just me. I also believe he has a purpose for your life, too, but you've got to show up and do the work. Walk your unique path, and try not to compare it to someone else's path. You have a unique story and unique gifts, and I hope you find the courage to share those with others. As I told my boys this morning before I left for work, find the courage to be respectful and kind in everything you do today.

CONCLUSION

You've learned. You've grown. Now it's time to implement what you've gained.

As I mentioned in the introduction, nothing in this book is revolutionary or new. Sure, I've shared a unique perspective and my unique stories, but in the end, I've left you with a handful of key principles. These principles will help you build a great life, a life you love.

It's not about taking the cold shower or drinking the green juice. Sure, certain practices can certainly help us on our paths, but they are ultimately meaningless unless they lead us to real change. When you want real change, the quick-fix solution won't cut it. You'll need a day-in, day-out, little bit each day, solution.

Think of your life and business as an adventure, and give

yourself to this moment rather than binding yourself to the past or the future.

As you show up, as you create, you'll find a secret power that wasn't so secret after all. Cheers to your journey.

If I can help with anything, send me a message at nick-dancer@dancerconcrete.com.

ABOUT THE AUTHOR

NICK DANCER owns and operates Dancer Concrete Design, a specialty concrete finishing company that started in his basement and has grown to be the leader for architectural concrete finishes in the region. He lives in Fort Wayne, Indiana, and his favorite thing is celebrating life with his wife, Alexis, and three sons.